Anatomy of the Perfect Golf Swing
The Surest Way to Better Golf

Glennon E. Bazzle

Illustrated by Sean Haynes
Photographed by Gus Bennett

Published by Lobdell and Potter
6900 Curran Road
New Orleans, LA 70126

Copyright 1998 by Glennon E. Bazzle

All rights reserved. No part of this book may be reproduced, stored in retrieval systems or transmitted in any form, by any means, including mechanical, electronic, photocopying, recording, or otherwise without prior written permission of the author.

Anatomy Of The Perfect Golf Swing, The Surest Way To Better Golf
Glennon E. Bazzle

Illustrator: Sean Haynes

Photographer: Gus Bennett

ISBN 0-9667079-0-7

Library of Congress Catalog Card Number: 98-96587

Third Printing, May, 2000

Published by Lobdell and Potter
6900 Curran Road
New Orleans, LA 70126

About the Author

Glennon E. Bazzle is nationally known and respected master masseur/fitness instructor with 39 years of experience. He is well-trained in massage therapy and has received diplomas and certificates in a variety of healing and massage therapy specialties.

His training and experience include:

- Shiatsu - Tulane University - New Orleans, Louisiana

- The Art of Scientific Spa Therapy - San Diego, California

- American School of Holistic Massage- West Palm Beach, Florida

- Membership-Alliance of Massage Therapists, Inc., New York, New York

- Medical Specialist- Louisiana Army National Guard

Mr. Bazzle's impressive educational background is complemented by a most prestigious history of working with the nation's finest hotel spas and resort areas. These include:

- Head Masseur, Jewish Community Center- New Orleans, Louisiana

- Regency Hotel Spa - Miami Beach, Florida

- Sun Spa and Hotel - Hollywood, Florida

- Riviera Hotel - Las Vegas, Nevada

- Rancho La Costa Hotel Spa and Resort - Carlsbad, California

- Independent Masseur with private clientele in New York, New York and Beverly Hills, California

He is also a certified teaching pro/member of the United States Golf Teachers Federation.

His extensive knowledge of the human body combined with his love for the game of golf produced this extraordinary work.

*Dedicated to
my wonderful Mother and Father,
Cleothilde J. and Thomas T. Bazzle,
in gratitude
for their many sacrifices and great example –*

TABLE OF CONTENTS

ACKNOWLEDGMENTS .... Page iii
FORWARD BY GLENNON E. BAZZLE .... Page iv
BODY PLANES AND ANATOMICAL POSITIONS AND DIRECTIONS .... Page vi
INTRODUCTION .... Page 1
A SHORT REVIEW OF THE BODY .... Page 4
    The Articulations of the Joints .... Page 6
HOW TO CREATE CENTRIFUGAL FORCE ON YOUR CENTER OF GRAVITY .... Page 8
    THE BACK-UPWARD SWING .... Page 8
    The Pelvic Girdle .... Page 8
        Prime Movers of the Hip Joint .... Page 10
    Exercise No. 1 .... Page 13
    Exercise No. 2 .... Page 16
    The Spine .... Page 17
        Prime Movers of the Spine .... Page 17
    The Pectoral Girdle .... Page 20
    The Sterno-Clavicular Articulation .... Page 21
        Prime Movers of the Sterno-Clavicular Joint ..... Page 22
    Exercise No. 3 .... Page 24
    Exercise No. 4 .... Page 26
    The Shoulder Joint .... Page 28
        Prime Movers of the Shoulder Joint .... Page 28
    Exercise No. 5 .... Page 31
    The Elbow Joint .... Page 32
        The Articulations of the Elbow .... Page 32
    The Forearm .... Page 33
        The Radio-Ulnar Articulation .... Page 34
        Prime Movers of the Forearm .... Page 34
THE SEVEN-DIGIT GRIP .... Page 36
        Forearm Prime Movers in the Grip .... Page 37
    The Hand .... Page 38
        Prime Movers of the Hand in the Grip .... Page 38
    Exercise No. 6 .... Page 43
    Exercise No. 7 .... Page 45
        Correct Left Hand Grip .... Page 45
        Correct Right Hand Grip .... Page 46
    Exercise No. 8 .... Page 48
    The Inferior Radio-Ulnar Articulation .... Page 51
        Prime Movers of Wrists in Back-Upward Swing .. Page 52

**HOW TO RELEASE CENTRIFUGAL FORCE ON YOUR
CENTER OF GRAVITY** .... Page 58
    THE DOWN-FORWARD SWING .... Page 58
        The Trapezius .... Page 56
        The Latissimus Dorsi .... Page 58
        The Teres Major .... Page 58
        The Posterior Fibers of the Deltoid .... Page 59
        The Triceps Brachii .... Page 60
        The Extensor Carpi Ulnaris .... Page 61
        The Flexor Carpi Ulnaris .... Page 62
THE MENTAL ASPECT OF THE GOLF SWING ...... Page 65
THE BIG TRICK .... Page 67
**HOW TO SYNTHESIZE THE BACK-UPWARD SWING
AND THE DOWN-FORWARD SWING** .... Page 69
    THE BACK-UPWARD SWING .... Page 69
    THE DOWN-FORWARD SWING .... Page 71
GLOSSARY OF KEY TERMS .... Page 77
REFERENCE .... Page 78

LIST OF ILLUSTRATION

FIGURE 1a:	The Body Planes and Anatomical Positions and Directions	Page vii
FIGURE 1b:	The Human Skeleton	Page 5
FIGURE 2:	The Pelvic Girdle	Page 9
FIGURE 3:	Prime Movers of the Right Hip Joint (Stabilizers of the Hip)	Page 10
FIGURE 4:	Prime Movers of the Right Hip Joint (Lateral Rotators of the Hip)	Page 12
FIGURE 5:	Prime Movers of the Spine (Rotators on Left Side of Spine)	Page 19
FIGURE 6:	The Pectoral Girdle	Page 20
FIGURE 7:	Prime Movers of the Sterno-Clavicular Joint (Move Left Shoulder Forward)	Page 22
FIGURE 8:	Bones of the Upper Left Extremity (The Shoulder Joint)	Page 27
FIGURE 9:	Prime Movers of the Shoulder Joint in the Back-Upward Swing	Page 29
FIGURE 10:	Prime Mover of the Shoulder Joint in the Back-Upward Swing	Page 30
FIGURE 11:	Prime Mover of the Shoulder Joint in the Back-Upward Swing	Page 30
FIGURE 12a:	Forearm Prime Mover of the Thumb in the Grip	Page 37
FIGURE 12b:	Forearm Prime Mover of the Fingers in the Grip	Page 37
FIGURE 12c:	Forearm Prime Mover of the Fingers in the Grip	Page 37
FIGURE 13:	Prime Movers of the Hand in the Grip	Page 40

FIGURE 14:	Prime Movers of the Hand in the Grip	Page 42
FIGURE 15:	Prime Movers of the Forearm in the Back-Upward Swing (Pronators)	Page 50
FIGURE 16a:	Prime Mover of the Wrist in the Back-Upward Swing	Page 53
FIGURE 16b:	Prime Mover of the Wrist in the Back-Upward Swing	Page 53
FIGURE 16c:	Prime Mover of the Wrist in the Back-Upward Swing	Page 54
FIGURE 17:	Prime Mover of the Shoulder in the Down-Forward Swing	Page 57
FIGURE 18:	Prime Movers of the Arm in the Down-Forward Swing	Page 59
FIGURE 19:	Prime Mover of the Forearm in the Down-Forward Swing	Page 61
FIGURE 20a:	Prime Movers of the Wrist in the Down-Forward Swing	Page 62
FIGURE 20b:	Prime Mover of the Wrist in the Down-Forward Swing	Page 63

LIST OF PHOTOGRAPHS

EXERCISE NO. 1
      Photos No. 1-2 .... Page 14
      Photos No. 3-4 .... Page 15

EXERCISE NO. 2
      Photos No. 5-6 .... Page 16

EXERCISE NO. 3
      Photos No. 7-8 .... Page 25

EXERCISE NO. 4
      Photos No. 9-10 .... Page 26

EXERCISE NO. 5
      Photos No. 11-12 .... Page 31

EXERCISE NO. 6
      Photo No. 13 .... Page 43
      Photos No. 14-16 .... Page 44

EXERCISE NO. 7
      Photo No. 17 .... Page 45
      Photos No. 18-20 .... Page 47

EXERCISE NO. 8
      Photos No. 21-22 .... Page 48
      Photo No. 23 .... Page 49

SYNTHESIZING THE PERFECT GOLF SWING
      Photos No. 24-27 .... Page 73
      Photos No. 28-31 .... Page 74
      Photos No. 32-35 .... Page 75

Acknowledgments

First I would like to thank all the individuals who read or listened to me read this book at various stages. Second I must express my sincere appreciation to those who actively participated in bringing this book into fruition. Namely: Allen and Louella Copeland, Gail T. Marigny, Tommie L. Roberson Jr., Sean Haynes, Gus Bennett and Dennis Joseph. And last but not least my deepest heartfelt gratitude to Myrna M. Moline for her confidence, encouragement and untiring and unwavering support and to whom I am forever indebted.

Forward
By Glennon E. Bazzle

"It Don't Mean A Thing If You Ain't Got That Swing". I don't know whether Duke Ellington had golf on his mind when he composed that song, but I do know that the phrase is quite accurate when it comes to the golf swing. I also know that the body did not need golf to be invented in order to make the movements necessary to properly swing a golf club.

This book was written for two reasons. One reason was the health of golfers. With over 39 years of health/fitness experience working at country clubs, hotels and resorts nationally, I have seen enough golf related injuries to last a life time. Ironically, most of the injuries were to muscles that are unnecessary in making the swing. And the other reason was the health of golf instructions. This was a reaction to a magazine article that stated," after 600 years of golf instructions, and with all its gurus and their technical wizardry, fewer than half of the world's players can regularly break a 100. Another irony is that if golf instructions had to be graded it would get an "I" for "incomplete".

Most golf instructors are dedicated to having the student approach the game mainly from the physical aspect of the sport. The student is given a club and told to perform the swing without any knowledge of the muscles and joints involved in making the movement. This can be very harmful for the student. Not only because of the possible physical injuries, but also because of the emotional and mental frustrations that come from not seeing any improvement in his or her game.

For the first time a book is designed that golfers, from beginners to professionals to instructors, can actually improve their performances by understanding a few simple principles of how the body really functions. This easy-reading, splendidly illustrated guide comes with a complete set of photographs, demonstrating each exercise as you go along plus the synthesizing of the swing at the end. The perfect application of these principles is the surest way to playing better golf immediately and permanently.

The golf swing as described herein is for the full swing for the right handed player. Left handers should do the reverse. **Tip:** Left handers should try playing from the right side since it is the muscles on the left side that create the power. The reason is that those muscles are usually already stronger. Right handers should also consider playing from the left side for the very same reason. The golf swing is the same for male or female, short or tall, thin or stout, young or old.

Here are some of the things you will learn and some of their benefits.

- The mechanical and anatomical principles used to execute a successful swing.

- The proper muscles, tendons, bones, joints and ligaments to use.

- Exercises to develop the proper muscles in the proper sequence used in the swing.

- How to relax emotionally, mentally and physically while playing golf.

- How to get more pleasure and enjoyment from the game of golf.

- Everything necessary to play good golf is contained right within your own body.

Some benefits of learning the **Perfect Golf Swing.**

- Create more accurate shots

- Improve scores immediately

- Increase confidence and self-esteem

- Save time and money and have more fun

- Success brings self-satisfaction

- Win recognition, praise and admiration

- Peace of mind, enjoyment and contentment await you

BODY PLANES

1. Median- Midline divides the body into right and left halves.

2. Frontal- This plane divides the body into equal front and back parts.

3. Transverse - This planes divides the body into upper and lower parts.

ANATOMICAL POSITIONS AND DIRECTIONS

4. Superior- Refers to a structure closer to the head or higher than another structure in the body.

5. Inferior- Refers to a structure closer to the feet or lower than another structure in the body.

6. Anterior- Refers to a structure more in front than another structure in the body.

7. Posterior- Refers to a structure more in back than another structure in the body.

8. Medial- Refers to a structure closer to the median plane than another structure in the body.

9. Lateral- Refers to a structure further away from the median plane than another structure in the body.

10. Proximal- Refers to a structure closer to the median plane or root of the limb than another structure in the limb. **Used in reference to limbs only.**

11. Distal- Refers to a structure further away from the median plane or root of the limb than another structure in the limb. **Used in reference to limbs only.**

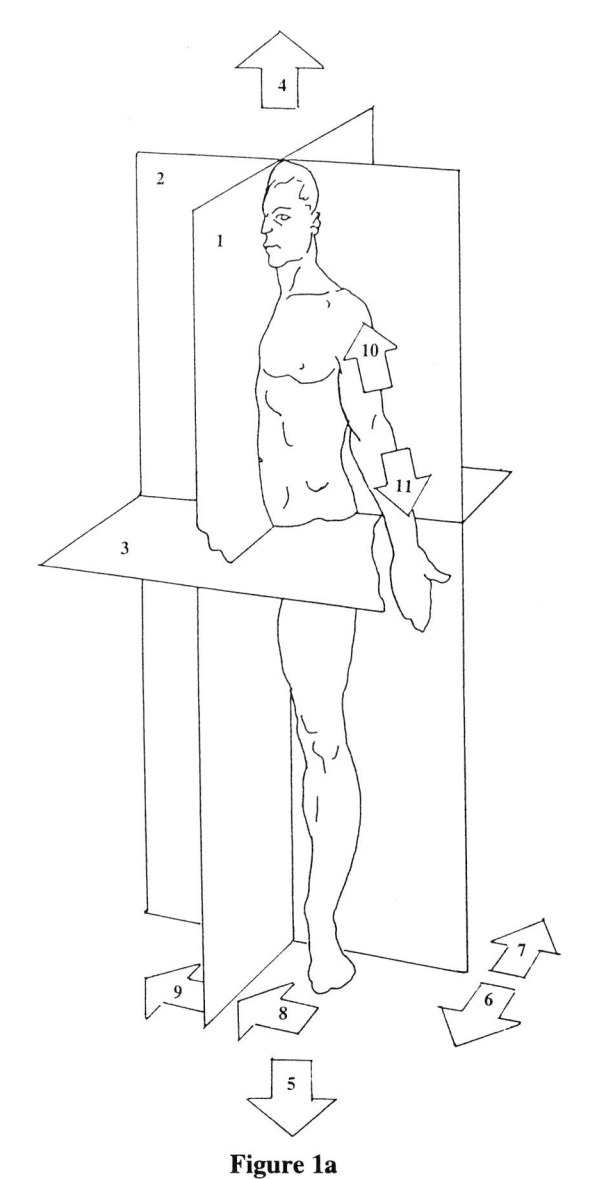

Figure 1a

Anatomy of The Perfect Golf Swing
The Surest Way To Better Golf
By Glennon E. Bazzle

Some golfers have been fortunate enough to discover a unique and successful swing by themselves through intuition. It is a successful swing because it gives them a chance to play their best golf consistently. Now you too can achieve your greatest golfing potentials and accomplishments without relying upon a chance discovery or an accidental stroke of luck. By demystifying the golf swing the author has reduced luck to a science. A science that any golfer can master when it is applied diligently, persistently and in the right spirit.

Most instructional golf books focus on the various aspects of playing the game of golf. Example: Driving, putting, chipping, sand shots, etc. The photographs and illustrations in this book show the scientific techniques created and designed by the author to give golfers the knowledge of the specific bones, joints and muscles of the body needed in making the **perfect golf swing**. You will learn how these muscles work in a logical, systematical and progressive technique. The principles and skills to apply them are attainable through study, observation and practice. By the conscious use of these principles and skills and your creative imagination you too can produce a successful swing consistently. Peace of mind, enjoyment and contentment await you, once you know the sequence of movements and observe them faithfully. Yesterday, knowing little about the golf swing you could only make an occasional lucky hit. Tomorrow, knowing much about the golf swing you will be able to fulfill your potentials and appreciate your accomplishments more as your score improves along with your confidence and self-esteem. Improvements come from confidence and confidence comes from knowledge. **"YOUR KNOWLEDGE OF THE PRINCIPLES AND THE SKILLS NEEDED TO APPLY THEM CREATES POWER."**

The format of this book is a short review of how the bones and muscles of the body work. The two parts of the golf swing, the **Back-Upward Swing** and the **Down-Forward Swing** are analyzed. The bones and joints involved in each part of the swing, and the muscles that pull them, are also analyzed. Each section of the **Back-Upward Swing** has an exercise that trains or retrains the correct muscles to make the correct action at the correct time. Master these exercises as we go along, and at the end of the last section when we synthesize the swing you'll be amazed how simple the swinging motion really is.

First we have to establish a central theme or a fulcrum from which to work around. Let me define what we will be doing. We will be swinging a golf club. Thus, the definition of the **perfect** golf swing. **The perfect golf swing is one complete, smooth, flowing motion without any emotional, mental or physical interruptions**.

The emotional and mental aspects are prerequisites to the physical aspects. There is no question whatsoever that our emotions are the single most important factors in our ability and attitude in handling the skill of the golf swing. The more we control our emotions, the more successful swings we make. Considerable effort is required however, at least initially, to train or retrain this special group of muscles to work together.

An *important point* is that swinging a golf club is a "global" skill, meaning a "whole skill", requiring only a limited set of basic components. Bowling, swimming, bike riding and walking are global skills also. Each component has a special job or skill to perform. Once you learn the components' skills and integrate them into a whole you can make the **perfect golf swing.** You don't have to go on forever adding additional basic skills. With proper practice and refinement of the techniques, the basic components' skills become completely integrated into the smooth flow of the **perfect golf swing**. The good news is that in time, when it becomes automatic, you're in for many emotionally rewarding days playing golf. The proper mental understanding of how the components or parts of the body work together to perform the golf swing is attainable through minimal study and maximum practice. The psychologists refer to this process as "appreciation precedes execution", which means,"you have to know what to do before you can do it."

The system set forth here is based on how the muscles, joints, tendons and ligaments of the body work most efficiently to produce the whirling motion needed in the golf swing. You see, there's a certain group of muscles moving a certain group of joints in a certain sequence. Any omission, incompletion, or interruption of the steps in this sequence usually results in a faulty swing that produces an errant shot.

A SHORT REVIEW OF THE BODY

Since swinging a golf club is an action performed by the body it seems appropriate to start with a short review of the anatomy and physiology, or structure and function of the human body.

We all know how amazing the body is, but it is put together quite simply. (See Figure 1 b). The skeletal system is divided into two main groups. The axial skeleton which consists of the skull, the vertebral column, and the thorax. And the appendicular skeleton which consists of the upper and lower extremities. The upper are involved with the pectoral girdle and the lower are involved with the pelvic girdle. Directly in front of the vertebral column is the sternum (the breast bone) which also runs vertically but is considerably shorter than its rear counterpart.

The entire skeleton in the adult consists of 200 distinct bones. These bones are divided into four classes: *Long, Short, Flat, and Irregular.* We will focus mainly on the *Long* and *Flat* bones, with a brief look at the vertebrae, which are in the *Irregular* class. The **long bones** are found in the limbs, where they form a system of levers, which have to sustain the weight of the trunk and to give the power of locomotion. The bones of this class that are important to us are the *femur, clavicle, humerus, radius, ulna, metacarpal bones* and the *phalanges*. The principal job of the **flat bones** is either extensive protection or provision of broad surfaces for muscular attachments. The bones of this class that are important to us are the *os coxae, scapula, sternum and ribs*. For all practical purposes, these are the only bones used to make the **perfect golf swing**.

The Human Skeleton

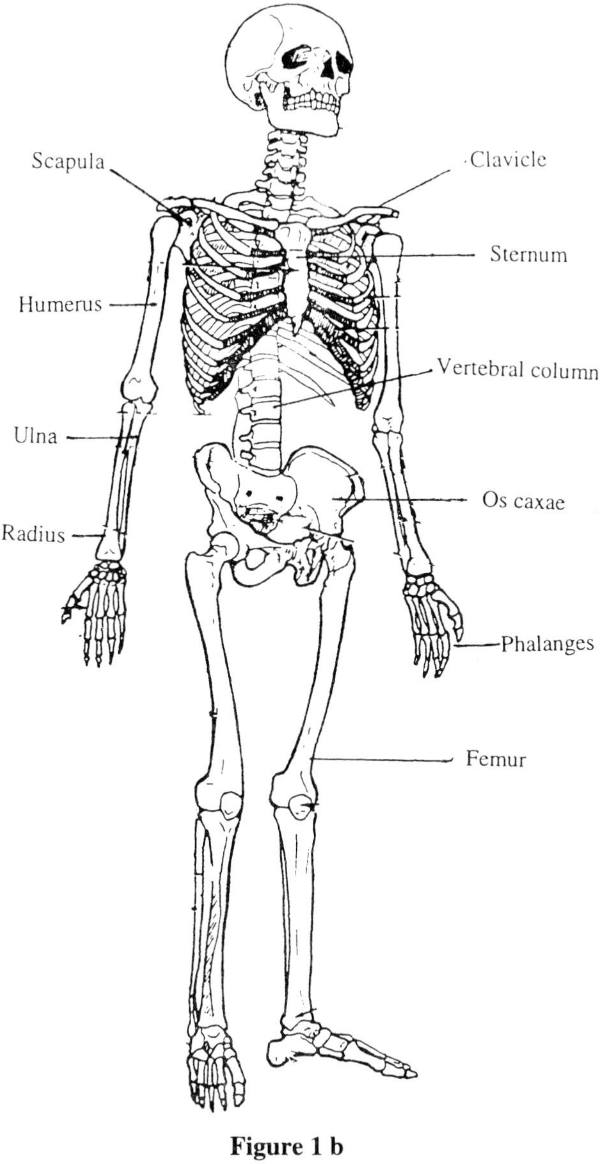

Figure 1 b
Bones to be analyzed in the golf swing.

The Articulations of the Joints

What is a joint? When two bones come together they form a joint. The movements of a joint are produced by organs known as skeletal muscles. Muscles rarely attach directly to the bones. When speaking of a muscle attaching to a bone, it is understood that a tendon or aponeurosis lies between the muscle and the bone.

There are more than 700 skeletal muscles in the human body. A muscle originates on one bone, crosses the joint and attaches to the other bone. When that muscle contracts it pulls the bone to which it is attached closer to the bone of origin, which stays stationary. Skeletal muscles and the bones to which they are attached operate on the lever principle.

A lever is a rigid bar that moves about a fixed point. To understand how a lever operates you must know these three things. One, the **Fulcrum,** the support or fixed point about which a lever turns. Two, the **Effort**, the force that moves the lever, and three, the **Resistance**, the weight that is overcome by the effort. The swinging of a **golf club** operates on the lever principle.

Usually a single muscle's primary function is to produce movement of a joint in a certain way. That muscle is called a **prime mover or Agonist.** However, to produce the refined movements that we make call for other muscles to take part also. They are the **Antagonist,** which opposes the action of the prime mover, and the **Synergis**t, a muscle that contracts and enhances the effectiveness of the prime mover by giving added strength, changing the angle of movement and/or holding one bone still so the other bone can move. As far as our subject matter is concerned, that of swinging a golf club, we will focus only on the prime movers of the joints.

Another principle on which the golf swing operates is centrifugal force.

I now give you the definition of centrifugal force and then satisfy the definition by applying it to the components of the body and their functions as used in making the **perfect golf swing.**

Centrifugal force is the force that an object moving along a circular path exerts on the body constraining the object and that acts outwardly away from the center of rotation.

Example: A stone (club head) whirled about on the end of a string (arm and shaft) exerts centrifugal force on the string (you).

The action of the golf swing is like centrifugal force. The bones involved in the golf swing moving away from the center of rotation are the os coxae/femur, the dorsal vertebrae, the ribs, scapula, clavicle, sternum, humerus, radius, ulna, metacarpals and phalanges.

The joints these bones form also moving away from the center of rotation are the hip, spine, chest, shoulder, arm, forearm, wrist and fingers. Each joint and it's articulation is illustrated or photographed and explained later.

To make learning the muscles easier here are some of the characteristics for which they are named. They are usually named in regard to their location, shape, size, direction of their fibers, the number of heads, action, origin and insertion. Along with their abilities to conduct electrical impulses and respond to stimuli, muscles also have the ability to stretch, *extensibility;* the ability to contract, *contractility*, is well developed in muscle tissue; and *elasticity,* the ability to bounce back after "stretching" or "contraction".

The skeleton and the muscles that pull it are homologous, right and left halves, upper and lower halves, front and behind, inner and outer. Because of this unique design we can perform many, many actions.

The actions of the golf swing is unique also, because there is no other time we need to perform those actions in that particular sequence.

Since satisfying the definition of centrifugal force is our objective we must identify an axial, a center or fulcrum and move outwardly. The most central location is where the three imaginary lines that divide the body into right and left halves, upper and lower halves, and front and behind intersect. That point is your center of gravity, the third principle of the golf swing. **Center of gravity is that point in your body around which your weight is evenly distributed or balanced and may be assumed to act.**

Notice from the author

You must pay close attention here in order to grasp the concept. What you learn from here is how opposites of the body uniquely working together produce balance, leverage, harmony, timing, rhythm, tempo, accuracy and centrifugal force, most efficiently, on your center of gravity, **resulting in the perfect golf swing.**

HOW TO CREATE CENTRIFUGAL FORCE ON YOUR CENTER OF GRAVITY

THE BACK-UPWARD SWING

Let's begin at the pelvic girdle.

The **pelvic girdle** is formed by the *os coxae bone* and the *femur*. (See Figure 2). The os coxae is a large, irregularly shaped, flat bone that, together with the sacrum and coccyx, make up the pelvis. It is formed of three bones, the ilium, the ischium, and pubis, which become fused in the adult. The fusion of these three bones produce a cup-like cavity, the (acetabulum), situated near the middle of the outer surface of the bone, which articulate with the head of the femur.

The femur (or thigh bone) is the longest, largest, and strongest bone in the skeleton. The feature of the bone that is of interest to us is its prominent head on the proximal portion of the bone, which articulates with the acetabulum. (See Figure 2).

The Pelvic Girdle

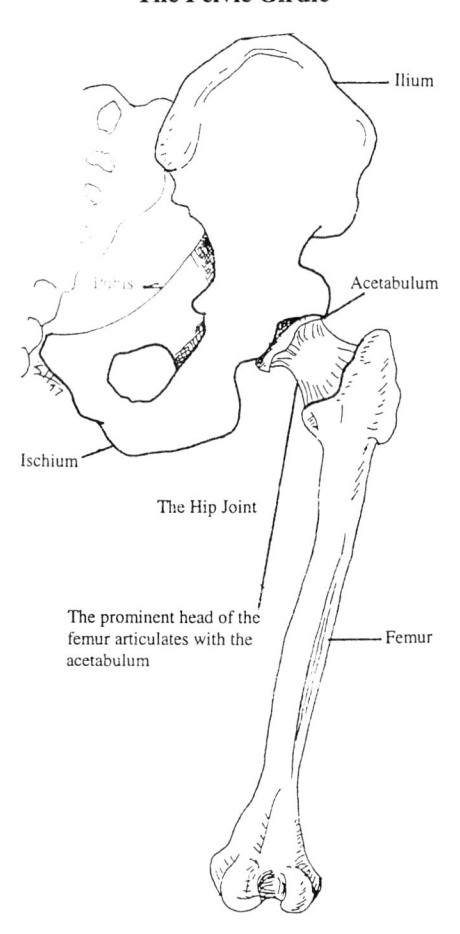

Figure 2

Prime Movers Of The Hip Joint

The prime movers of the hip in the golf swing are the Gluteus maximus and Gluteus medius (See Figure 3), and the Lateral Rotators (muscles that rotate the thigh outwardly). (See Figure 4)

Stabilizers of the Hip

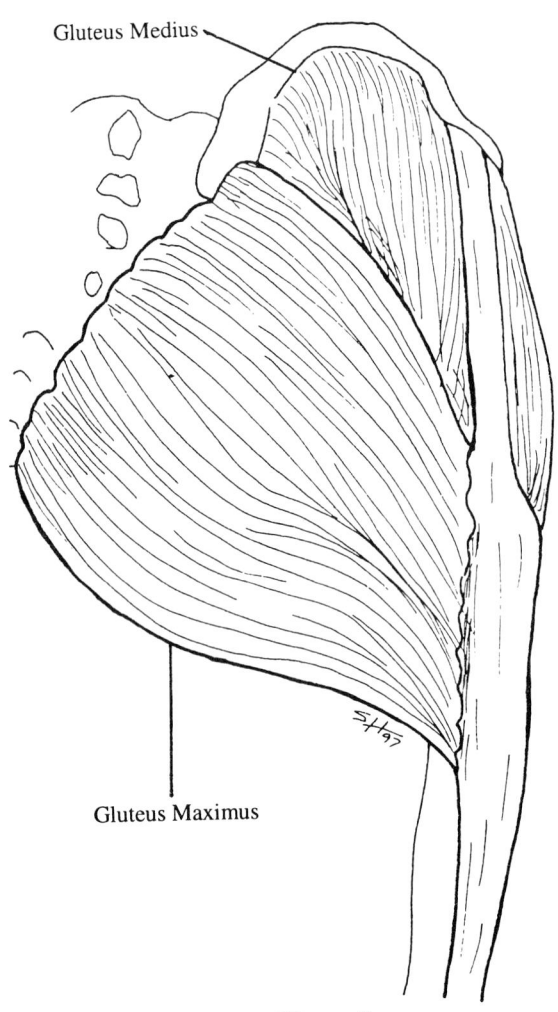

Figure 3

The **gluteus maximus,** the most superficial muscle in the gluteal region, is a very broad and thick, fleshy mass of quadrilateral shape, which forms the prominence of the buttocks. The muscle is extremely coarse and collected into large bundles. This structure is very powerful and helps with maintaining the trunk in the erect posture. It arises from the superior curved line of the ilium and from the posterior surface of the lower part of the sacrum. The fibers are directed obliquely downward and outward, terminate in a thick tendon, which is inserted into the outer thigh.

Action: Taking its fixed point from below, it acts upon the pelvis, supporting it and the whole trunk upon the head of the femur, which is especially obvious in standing on one leg. The lower part of the muscle also acts as a lateral rotator of the limb.

The **gluteus medius** is a broad, thick, radiated muscle, situated on the outer surface of the pelvis. It arises from the outer surface of the ilium. The fibers converge to a strong flattened tendon which is inserted into the outer surface of the great trochanter.

Action: The gluteus medius is called into action in supporting the body on one limb. It is also an important hip stabilizer and postural muscle because it keeps the hips level when walking or running.

The lateral rotators which include the **pyriformis,** the **obturator** (*externus* and *internus*), the **gemellus** (*superior* and *inferior*), and the **pectineus** all originate from different points on the os coxae and travel laterally to insert at different points on the head of the femur.

Action: Powerful lateral rotators.

Lateral Rotators of the Right Hip

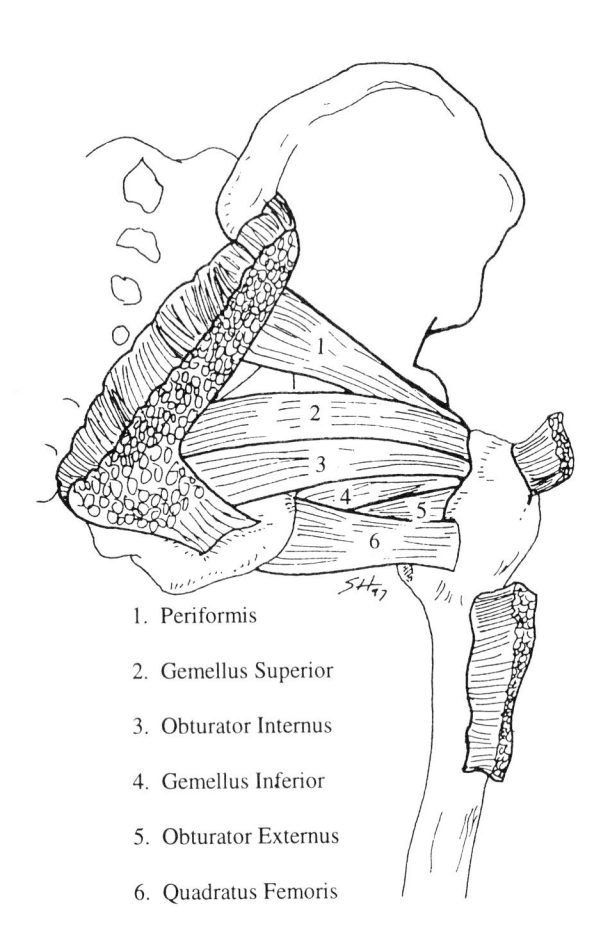

1. Periformis
2. Gemellus Superior
3. Obturator Internus
4. Gemellus Inferior
5. Obturator Externus
6. Quadratus Femoris

Figure 4

Now it is time to exercise these prime movers that stabilize and rotate the hip outwardly.

Exercise No.1: Establishing Correct Body Balance

By practicing this exercise, you will learn the proper action of the hips, legs and feet which goes along with the natural shifting of your weight. This paves the way for the proper coordination of the body, arms and hands in the swing.   **Photo 1.**

1) Stand erect in a normal position.

2) Place heels in a comfortable spread, about shoulder width, and toes pointed outward at about thirty degrees.

3) Face forward and aim your chin at a point directly opposite the center of your body.

4) Your head must be kept as still as possible. **Never move your chin.** Do not tilt it forward, backward or to either side.

5) Hold a club near each end, letting the shaft rest horizontally against your thighs.

6) Find your center of gravity. Without moving any part of the body above the waist, slightly bend your right knee. Your left leg should be straight and have about 75% of your weight balanced between the ball and heel of that foot, with a little more toward the inside of the heel. **Photo 2**.

7) Now shift your weight to the right leg having about 75% of your weight balanced between the ball and heel of that foot, with a little more toward the inside of the heel. **BEWARE!! The shifting**

motion is not a sway. It is the natural shifting of your weight. Like walking without moving your feet. Always feel about 75% of your weight balanced between the ball and heel of the foot of the straightened leg. You must feel it to know it.
See Photos 3 Front View & Photo 4 Rear View.

This is the first movement in the full swing and it establishes the solid foundation that is needed to create perfect balance and leverage. The balance and leverage allow you to generate maximum clubhead speed which translates into more distance and more efficient use of your energy. This exercise can be done anywhere, anytime you're standing.

You can never do too much of this exercise.

Exercise No. 1   Step 1-5   Photo 1

Exercise No. 1   Step 6   Photo 2

Exercise No. 1   Step 7   Photo 3
Front View

Exercise No. 1   Step 7   Photo 4
Rear View

NOTES:

Exercise No. 2
The Proper Hip Turn

Repeat steps 1 thru 5 of Exercise No.1   **Photo 1**

6) Find your center of gravity. Without moving any part of your body above the waist, shift your weight to the right leg then turn to the right using the right lateral rotators. **Photos 5 & 6.**

Exercise No. 2   Step 6   Photo 5
Front View

Exercise No. 2   Step 6   Photo 6
Rear View

The Spine

The **spine** is a flexuous and flexible column formed of a series of bones called *vertebrae* (from *vertere,* to turn). There are 33 in number, but we are interested in the 12 that make up the dorsal region. Each vertebra consists of two essential parts- an anterior solid segment or *body*, and a posterior segment or *arch.* The bodies of the vertebrae are piled one upon the other, forming a strong pillar for the support of the cranium and trunk. The 12 vertebrae of the dorsal region have transverse and spinous processes, which serve as levers for the attachment of muscles which move the different parts of the spine.

Prime Movers Of The Spine

The prime movers of the spine that we are interested in are the Multifidus spinae and the Rotatores spinae. (See Figure 5).

The **multifidus spinae** consist of a number of fleshy and tendinous fasciculi which fill up the groove on either side of the spinous processes of the vertebrae from the sacrum to the axis. The muscles of the dorsal region, that region between the lumbar and the axis, arise from the transverse processes. Each fasciculus, passing obliquely upward and inward, is inserted into the whole length of the spinous process of one of the vertebrae above.

Action: The Multifidus Spinae, besides preserving the erect position of the spine, serves to rotate it, so that the front of the trunk is turned to the side opposite to that from which the muscle acts.

The **rotatores spinae** are found only in the dorsal region of the spine, beneath the Multifidus spinae; they are eleven in number on each side. Each muscle is small and somewhat quadrilateral in form; it arises from the upper and back part of the transverse process, and is inserted into the lower border and outer surface of the lamina of the vertebrae above, the fibers extending as far inward as the root of the spinous process. The first is found between the first and second dorsal vertebrae, and the last, between the eleventh and twelfth.

Action: The Rotatores Spinae assists the Multifidus Spinae to rotate the spine, so that the front of the trunk is turned to the side opposite to that from which the muscle acts.

These muscles together with the muscles in the following section will prepare you for exercise number three.

Rotators on Left Side of Spine

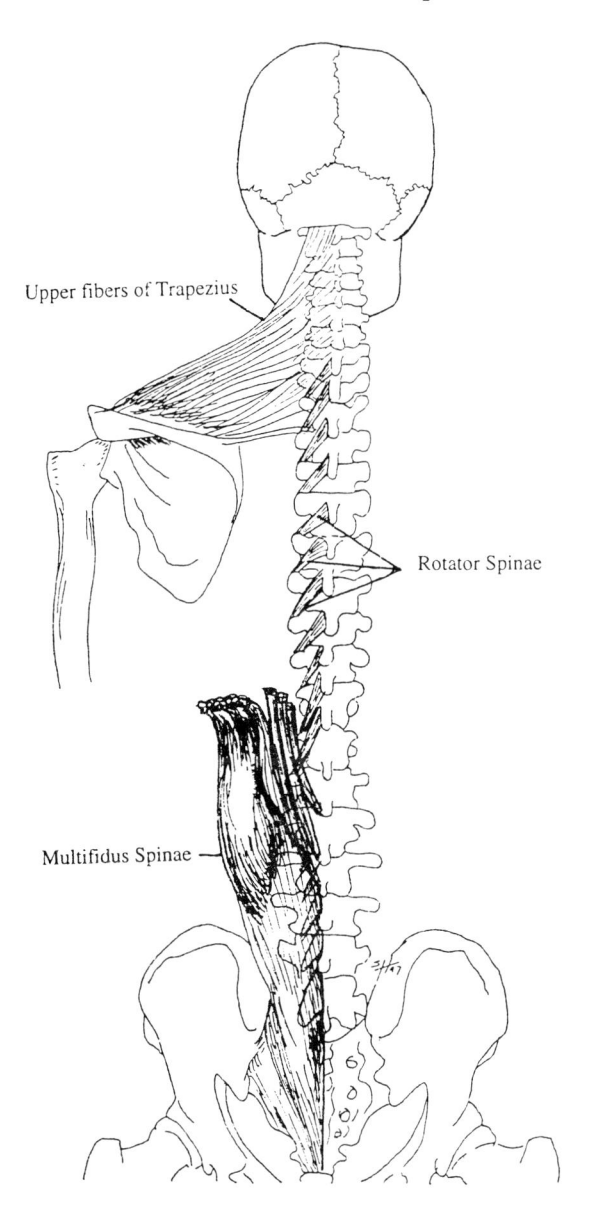

Figure 5

The Pectoral Girdle

The **pectoral girdle** consists of the *scapula* and the *clavicle* (commonly known as the shoulder blade and collar bone, respectively). (See Figure 6)

It is different in front and behind. In front, the girdle is completed by the upper end of the sternum, with which the inner extremities of the clavicle articulates. Behind, the girdle is widely imperfect and the scapula is connected to the trunk by muscles only. Together, the scapula and the clavicle anchor the upper extremities to the skeleton.

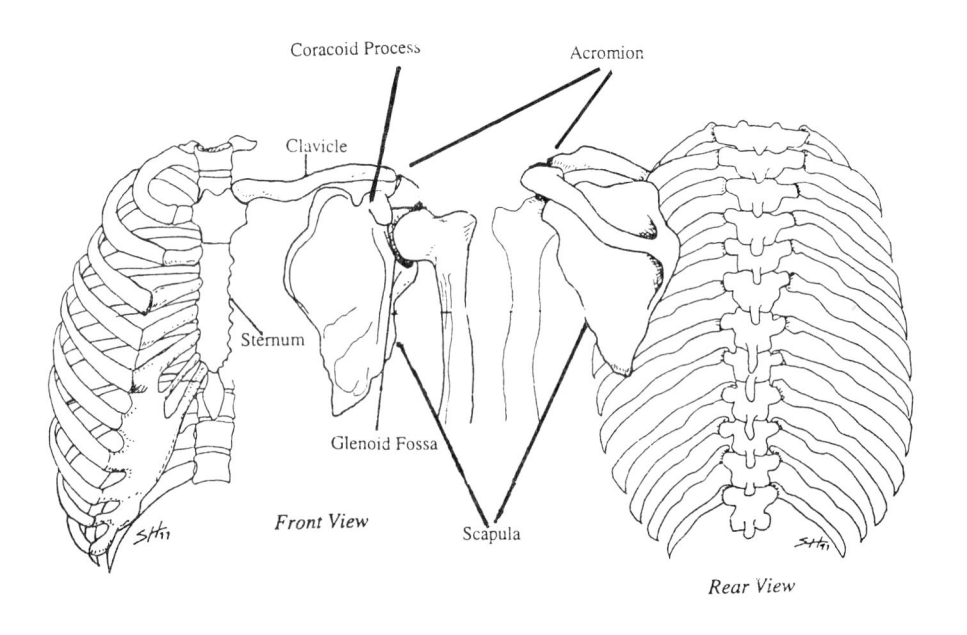

Figure 6

The **scapula**, or *shoulder blade*, is a large, flat bone, triangular in shape with its anterior surface facing the ribs, and its posterior surface exposed on the back of the body. The names of the three angles are, the superior, the inferior and the lateral. The names of the three borders or edges are, the superior, the medial and the lateral. Here are a few of the interesting features of the scapula. A ridge on the posterior surface of the bone is called the ***spine.*** The outer end of the spine is called the ***acromion***, which articulates with the clavicle. In front of the acromion is another prominent feature called the ***coracoid process***, a point where two of the 21 most important muscles in the golf swing are attached. On the lateral border of the scapula is the ***glenoid fossa,*** to which the humerus is attached.

The **clavicle**, (clavis: a key) or *collar bone*, forms the anterior portion of the shoulder girdle. It is a long bone, curved somewhat like the italic *f*, and placed nearly horizontally at the upper and the anterior part of the thorax, immediately above the first rib. It articulates by its inner extremity with the upper border of the sternum and by its outer extremity with the acromion process of the scapula serving to sustain the upper extremity in the various positions which it assumes, and at the same time it allows great latitude of motion in the arm.

The Sterno-Clavicular Articulation

Action: This articulation is the center of movement of the shoulder, and admits of a limited amount of motion in nearly every direction- upward, downward, backward, forward, as well as circumduction. When these movements take place in the joints, the clavicle in its motion carries the scapula with it, this bone gliding on the other motion of the chest. This joint, therefore, forms the center from which all movements of the supporting arch of the shoulder originate, and is the only point of articulation of this part of the skeleton with the trunk.

Prime Movers of the Sterno-Clavicular Joint

The prime movers of this joint are the Pectoralis Minor, the Serratus Anterior and the Upper Fibers of the left Trapezius. (See Figure 7).

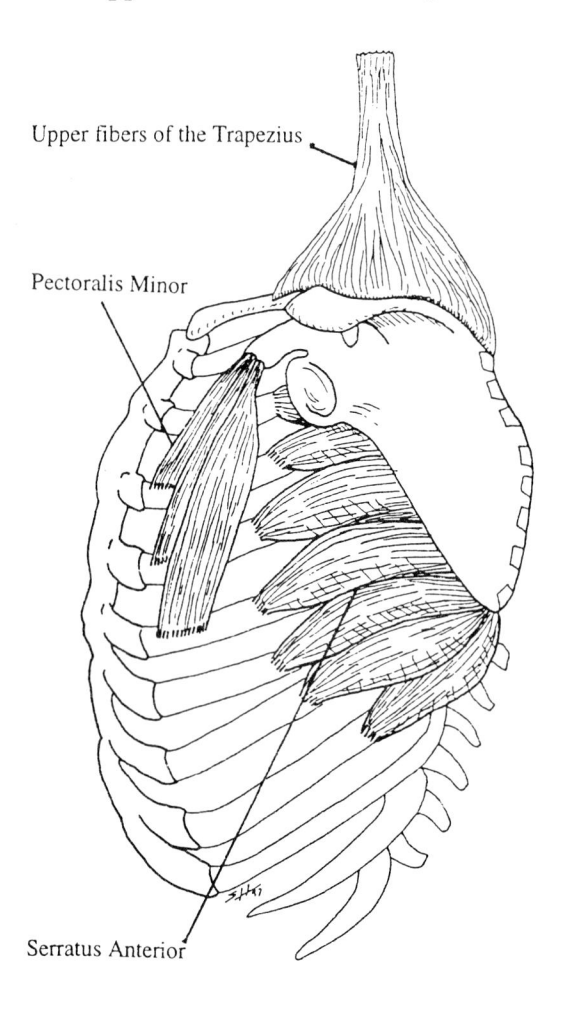

Figure 7

The **pectoralis minor** is a thin, flat triangular muscle situated at the upper part of the thorax, beneath the pectoralis major. It arises by three tendinous digitations from the upper margins and outer surfaces of the third, fourth, and fifth ribs near their cartilages. The fibers pass upward and outward and converge to form a flat tendon, which is inserted into the inner border and the upper surface of the coracoid process of the scapula.

Action: The pectoralis minor depresses the point of the shoulder, drawing the scapula downward and inward towards the thorax and throwing the inferior angle backward.

The **serratus anterior** is a thin, irregularly quadrilateral muscle, situated between the ribs and the scapula at the upper and lateral part of the chest. It arises from the outer surface and upper border of the eight upper ribs. From this extensive attachment the fibers which are closely applied to the chest-wall, pass backward to reach the medial border of the scapula.

Action: The serratus anterior, as a whole, carries the scapula forward, and at the same time raises the medial border of the bone. It is therefore concerned in the act of pushing. It works in concert with the pectoralis minor.

The **upper fibers of the left trapezius**, also shown in (Figure 5), cover the upper back part of the neck and shoulders. It arises from the inner third of the superior curved line of the occipital bone and the spinous process of the seventh cervical. The fibers proceed downward and outward, then insert into the outer third of the posterior border of the clavicle.

Action: If the head is held still the upper fibers will elevate the point of the shoulder, as in supporting weights.

Exercise No. 3: Proper Back and Chest Action in the Swing

Repeat Steps **1** through **5** of Exercise NO.1.

6) Find your center of gravity. Without moving any part of your body below your waist, turn your upper left torso and shoulder forward using the muscles of the spine and those just analyzed until the outer tip of the left shoulder comes under the chin. **Photo 7**

7) Remember: The clavicle is the KEY. After the Serratus anterior and the Pectoralis minor have protracted the shoulders, causing them to become somewhat rounded, the left rotators of the dorsal region of the spine are contracted, causing the front of the body to move forward and to the right. As that is happening the left serratus anterior, the left pectoralis minor and the upper fibers of the left trapezius are also contracting, causing the inner tip of the left collar bone to articulate with the sternum, and bringing the outer tip of the left collar bone directly under the chin. Reverse the action, bringing the tip of the right shoulder under the chin. **The spine and chin represent your midline, or the fulcrum on which you build centrifugal force.** You are turning on your midline so it must remain stabilized. If you lose your midline you lose your fulcrum. If you lose your fulcrum you lose your balance and leverage. If you lose your balance and leverage you lose your distance and accuracy. And if you lose your distance and accuracy you will shoot a very high number.
Photo 8

Exercise No. 3   Step 6   Photo 7

Exercise No. 3   Step 7   Photo 8

Exercise No. 4 Proper Right Hip and Left Shoulder Turn

The action is a combination of Exercises No. 2 and No. 3.

Repeat Steps **1** through **5** of Exercise No.1

6) Find your center of gravity. Slightly bend your right knee, having 75% of your weight balanced on your left leg.

7) Shift your weight to the right leg and rotate laterally. Make the proper left shoulder turn. Reverse the action. Repeat! Repeat! **Photos 9 & 10**

Exercise No. 4　　Step 7　Photo 9
Front View

Exercise No. 4　　Step 7　　Photo 10
Rear View

Bones of the Upper Left Extremity

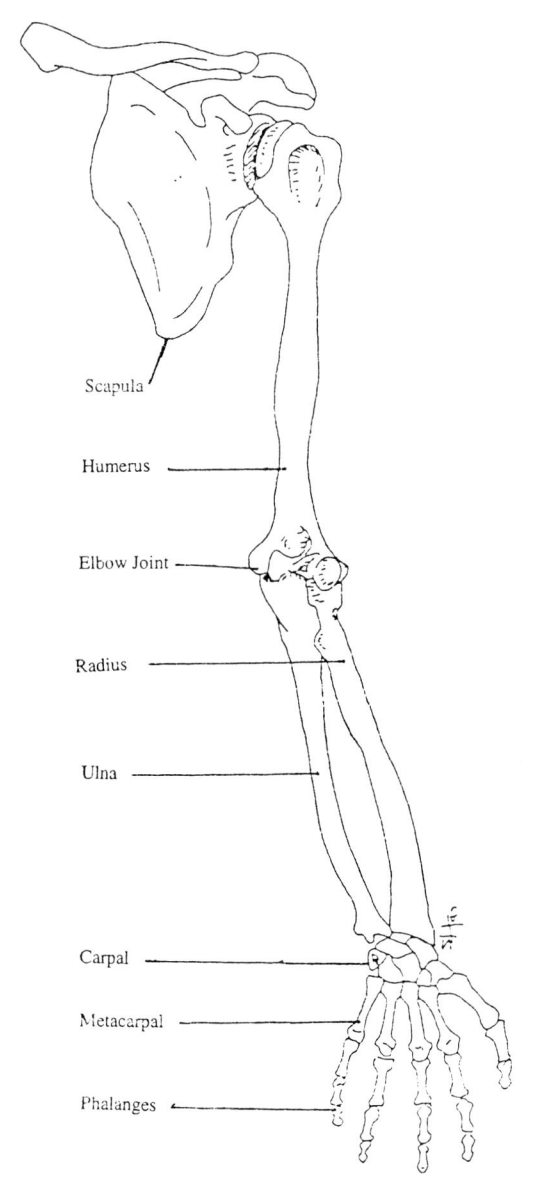

- Scapula
- Humerus
- Elbow Joint
- Radius
- Ulna
- Carpal
- Metacarpal
- Phalanges

Figure 8

The Shoulder Joint

The shoulder articulations are made by the head of the humerus and the glenoid cavity of the scapula. (See Figure 8).

The **humerus** is the longest and largest bone of the upper extremity. It has a shaft and two extremities. The upper end has a large rounded head, nearly hemispherical in form. It is directed upward, inward and a little backward, and articulates with the glenoid cavity of the scapula.

The lower end will be analyzed later.

Prime Movers Of The Shoulder Joint

In keeping with our premise, moving away from the center of rotation and focusing only on the prime movers, we will focus on the Coraco-Brachialis, the Anterior Fibers of the Deltoids in particular, and one group, the Musculotendinous Cuff, commonly known as the "Rotator Cuff", in general. Those are the muscles of concern for us at this point in the golf swing.

Let's look at the group first.

The **supraspinatus**, the **infraspinatus**, the **teres minor** and the **subscapularis** muscles collectively, make up the "rotator cuff". (See Figure 9).They are homologous to the lateral rotators of the femur. All of them originate on the scapula, travel laterally, to insert on the head of the humerus.

Action: The "rotator cuff" muscles are involved in every movement of the upper arm. Because of their points of insertions they provide a powerful protection against displacement of the head of the bone.

Figure 9

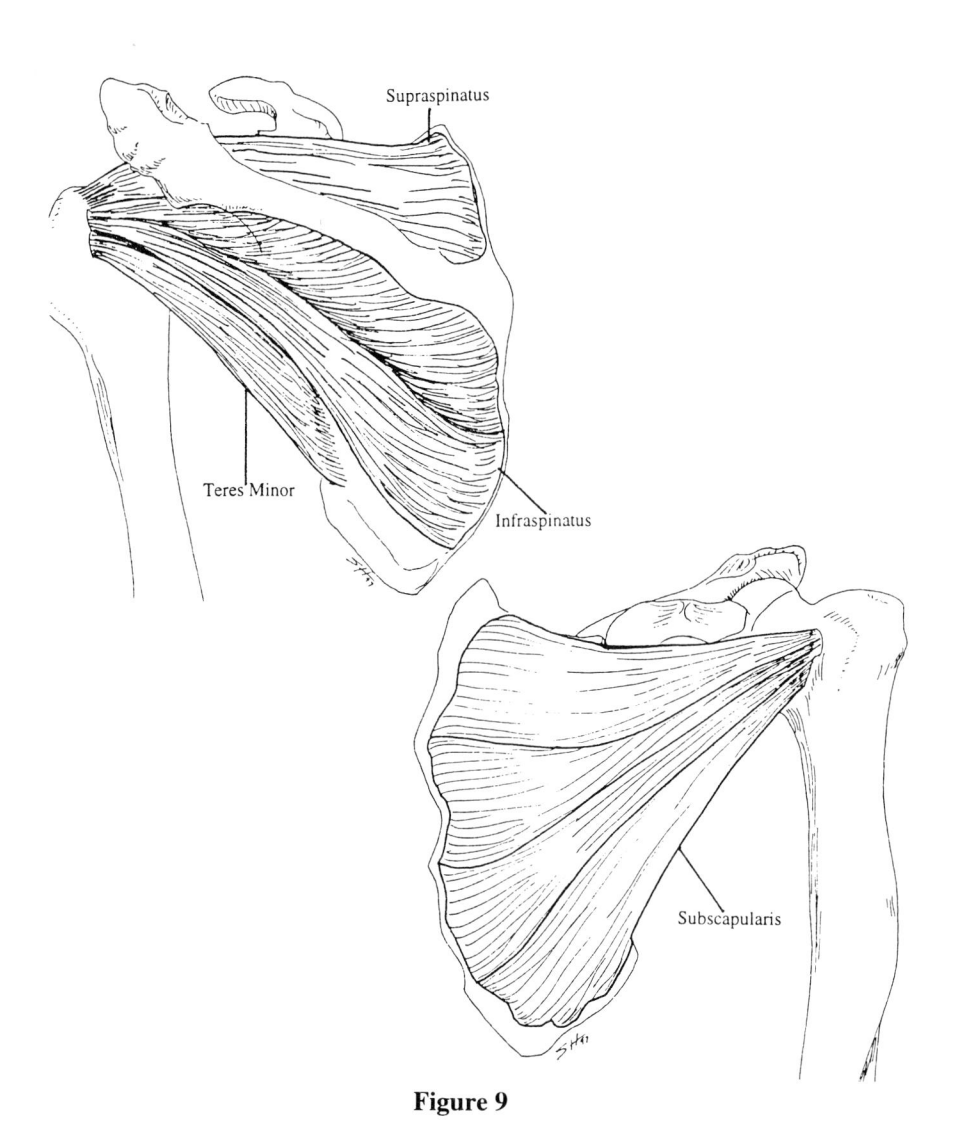

The **coraco-brachialis**, (See Figure 10), is a small muscle situated at the upper and inner part of the arm. It arises by fleshy fibers from the apex of the coracoid process. The fibers pass downward, backward, and a little outward, forming a flat tendon which is inserted into the medial shaft of the humerus. It is shown in relationship to the pectoralis minor.

Action: The coraco-brachialis draws the humerus forward and inward, and at the same time, assists in elevating it toward the scapula.

The anterior fibers of the deltoids. (See Figure 11). The deltoid is a large, thick, triangular muscle, which gives the rounded outline of the shoulder. It surrounds the shoulder-joint, covering it on its outer side, and in front and behind. It arises from the outer third of the anterior border and upper surface of the clavicle, and from the posterior border of the spine of the scapula. From this extensive origin the fibers converge toward their insertion, the middle passing vertically, the anterior obliquely, backward, and the posterior obliquely forward. They unite to form a thick tendon, which is inserted into the middle of the outer side of the shaft of the humerus. Right now we want the action of the anterior fibers.

Action: The anterior fibers acting alone causes flexion and medial rotation of the humerus.

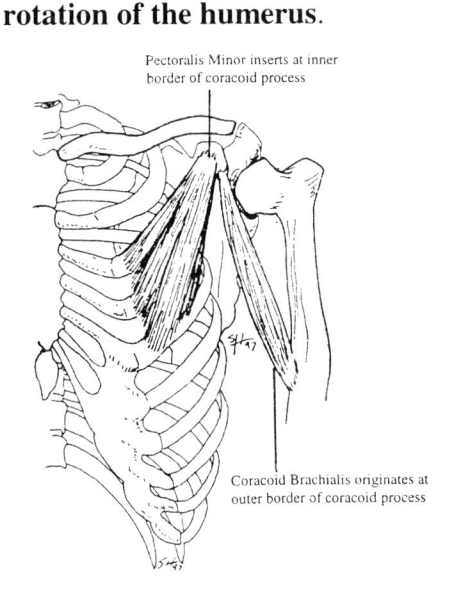

Figure 10

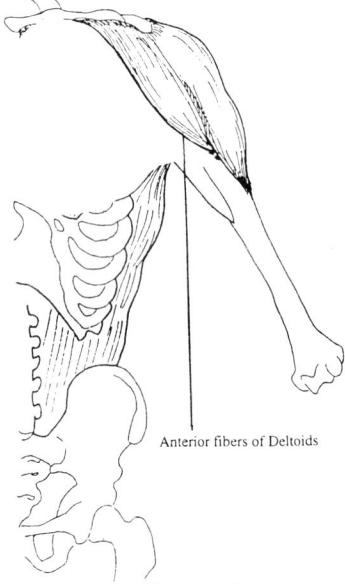

Figure 11

Exercise No. 5

1) Standing erect, simply raise your left arm extending it forward. Those are the muscles we've just analyzed. **Photo 11**

2) Repeat exercise NO. 4. When the left shoulder comes under the chin, raise the left arm. **Photo 12**

Exercise No. 5   Step 1   Photo 11

Exercise No. 5   Step 1   Photo 12

The Elbow Joint

The **elbow** is a *ginglymus or hinge joint.* (See Figure 8). The elbow joint comprises three different portions, namely, the joint between the ulna and humerus, that between the head of the radius and humerus, and that between the superior portions of the radius and the ulna.

The Articulations of the Elbow

The portion of the joint between the ulna and the humerus is a simple hinge joint, and allows for movement of flexion and extension only. The radial head of the humerus articulates with the cup-shaped depression on the head of the radius. The circumference of the head of the radius articulates with the lesser sigmoid cavity of the ulna, allowing for the movement of rotation of the radius on the ulna, the chief action of the radial ulna articulation. In combination with any position of flexion or extension, the head of the radius can be rotated in the upper radial joint, carrying the hand with it. The hand is articulated with the lower surface of the radius only.

You must admit that up to this point the golf swing is quite simple. We have analyzed and used two bones and three muscles at the lower right portion of the body; the spine and two of its muscles at the center of the body; three bones and three muscles of the upper left portion of the body and the upper left arm bone and two of its muscles. That's seven bones and ten muscles. Four joints, the hip, back, shoulder and upper left arm all turning independently, and in the proper sequence that makes it look like one smooth movement.

The Forearm

As we continue along our current, constant, logical, and systematical process of satisfying the definition of centrifugal force, moving away from the center of rotation, we come to the discussion of the lower part of the humerus and the forearm. The forearm is that portion of the upper extremity situated between the elbow and the wrist. Its skeleton is composed of two bones, the radius and ulna. (See Figure 8).

The **radius,** *a ray, or spoke of a wheel,* is a long bone situated on the outer side (thumb side) of the forearm lying side by side with the ulna. Its upper end is small, and forms only a small part of the elbow-joint; but its lower end is large, and forms the chief part of the wrist. The *head* is of cylindrical form depressed on its upper surface into a shallow cup which articulates with the radial head of the humerus. Around the circumference of the head is a smooth, articular surface which articulates with the lesser sigmoid cavity of the ulna. This spinning action causes rotation of the forearm. The lower end of the radius is large, and of quadrilateral form, and provided with two articular surfaces. One at the extremity, for articulation with the carpus, and one at the inner side of the bone, for articulation with the ulna.

The **ulna** is a long bone placed at the inner side of the forearm, parallel with the radius. It is the larger and longer of the two bones. Its upper extremity, of great thickness and strength, forms a large part of the articulation of the elbow-joint. It has two large, curved processes, the *olecranon* process and the *coronoid* process; and two concave, articular cavities, the greater and lesser sigmoid cavities. The olecranon process sticks out when the forearm is bent, and fits perfectly into the olecranon fossa of the humerus when the forearm is straightened, *"locking the elbow"*. The lower extremity of the ulna is very small and does not articulate with the wrist-joint. The distal end of the bone has two projections, the head (which articulates with the radius) and the styloid process.

The Radio-Ulnar Articulation

The articulation of the radius with the ulna is effected by ligaments which connect together both extremities as well as the shafts of these bones. They may, consequently, be sub-divided into three sets: 1) the superior radio-ulnar, which is a portion of the elbow joint; 2) the middle radio-ulnar; and 3) the inferior radio-ulnar articulation. We will consider the superior and the inferior portions.

The superior articulation is a pivot joint. The bones entering into its formation are the inside of the circumference of the head of the radius rotating within the lesser sigmoid cavity of the ulna. Its only ligament is the annular or orbicular. The orbicular ligament is a strong, flat band of ligamentous fibers which surrounds the head of the radius and retains it in firm connection with the lesser sigmoid cavity of the ulna.

Joint Action

The movement which takes place in this articulation is limited to rotation of the head of the radius within the orbicular ligament and upon the lesser sigmoid cavity of the ulna, rotation forward being called pronation; rotation backward, called supination.

The Prime Movers Of The Forearm

Now here comes the fun part of the golf swing. The two bones of the forearm we just analyzed have ten prime movers. Three that are used in the grip; two that pronate the arm; three that cock the wrist in the up-backward swing; and two that uncock the wrist at impact. Multiply that by two.

Let's begin with the three used in the grip and include the muscles of the hands that are also used in the grip. We will return to the other forearm prime movers later.

Before we get to the grip I think this is the best time to introduce you to another action that muscles make. It is called **circumduction**, the fourth and final principle on which the golf swing operates. You are probably familiar with the meanings of the following terms which also describe the actions that the muscles make. They are: **rotation**-to spin or turn; **flexion**- to decrease the angle of a joint; **extension**- to increase the angle of a joint; **adduction**- to bring toward the body; and **abduction**- to move away from the body.

So what in the world is circumduction? **Circumduction is a combination of all of the other actions. (A great example is throwing a ball underhand). Besides being a combination of all the other actions, the most unique thing about circumduction is that while it's being performed the distal end moves in a circular path.** Then applied to the golf swing, the distal end is the clubhead. The path of the clubhead, the position of the club face and the speed its traveling when it passes the bottom of its arc are of utmost importance. The controlling factor that determines the path of the club head, the position of the club face and the speed it travels is the grip.

THE SEVEN DIGIT GRIP

The word **"grip"** is defined in Webster's as **the act of taking firmly and holding fast with the hands**. The proper placing of the hands on the golf club is called the **"proper grip"**. The proper grip is based on the fact that both hands and their fingers must be placed on the club in such a manner that both wrists are allowed to make the same action at the same time.

There are four different directions in which the wrists can move. Really, two pairs of opposite directions. There is palmar flexion and dorsal flexion. **Example:** Motion made waving good-bye. And there is radial flexion and ulnar flexion. **Example:** Motion made hammering.

We need the latter in making the full golf swing.

(Note: The dorsal and palmar flexion action is used in putting and chipping, but this is done with stiff wrists and there is no actual flexion taking place).

However, at this point I'm asking you to recall two things that were written in the earlier sections of the book. One was that I promised to show you a systematical, logical, and physically efficient method of swinging a golf club. And the other was that we are beings with four extremities. The latter is true, except for when we are required to hold one thing in both hands at the same time. When we do, we become beings with three extremities. So, in order to assume the proper grip we must first admit that we have temporarily changed, anatomically, into a three extremity being. Our new temporary body would and does look like this. Two lower limbs (legs), whose soles are on the ground, and one upper limb made of two arms attached to one **"new"** hand.

Our one **"new"** hand has the little finger, the ring finger, and the middle finger and thumb of the left hand, and the middle finger, index finger and thumb of the right hand. Emphasis should be placed on positioning these **SEVEN DIGITS** properly on the club and maintaining an adequate and consistent amount of pressure through out the swing.

Thus by gripping the club properly, the face of the club becomes the perfect extension of the "new" hand in which to throw the ball underhand style. **Note: When the hands work together as a single unit, it is then, and only then, that the distal end of circumduction can be achieved consistently, purposely, confidently, and efficiently.**

Forearm Prime Movers In The Grip

The prime movers in the forearm used in the grip are the Flexor Pollicis Longus, (FPL); the Flexor Sublimis Digitorum, (FSD); and the Flexor Profundus Digitorum (FPD). (See Figures 12a, 12b and 12c).

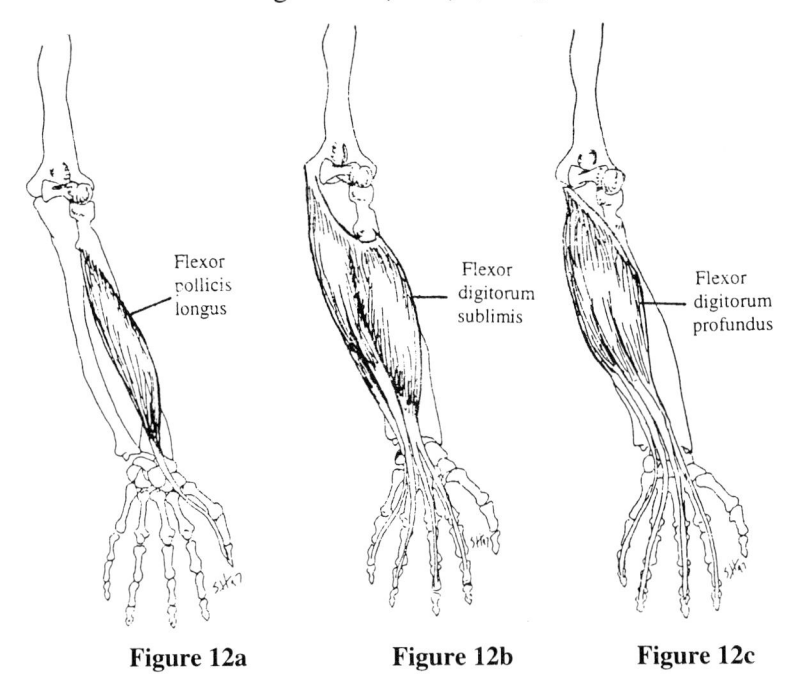

Figure 12a — Flexor pollicis longus

Figure 12b — Flexor digitorum sublimis

Figure 12c — Flexor digitorum profundus

The **flexor muscles** of both forearms are involved in the closing of the fingers around the club. All of these muscles originate on the ulna bone. They travel downward on the inner surface of the forearm and terminate at or near the end of the fingers.

Action: The "FPL" terminates at the end of the thumb and is a flexor of the phalanges of the thumb. The "FSD" terminates at the second to last bones of the fingers and flexes first the middle and then the approximal phalanx. The " FPD " terminates at the last bones of the fingers and is one of the flexors of the phalanges.

Note: After the flexor sublimis has bent the second phalanx, the flexor profundus flexes the terminal one, but it cannot do so until after the contraction of the superficial muscle.

The Hand

The skeleton of the hand is subdivided into three segments- the Carpus or wrist bones; the Metacarpus or bones of the palm; and the Phalanges or bones of the digits. We will look at the latter two divisions. The metacarpal bones are five in number and are long cylindrical bones. Each bone has its own peculiar characteristics and serves as attachment points for as little as three to as many as six muscles each. The phalanges are the long bones of the fingers; they are fourteen in number, three for each finger, and two for the thumb. They serve as attachment points for at least two to as many as five muscles each.

Prime Movers Of The Hand In The Grip

The prime movers of the hand used in gripping the club are the Opponens Minimi Digiti, the Opponens Pollicis, the Flexor Minimi Digiti Brevis, the Flexor Pollicis Brevis, the Adductor, the first Dorsal Interosseus and the Palmar Interossei.

The **opponens minimi digiti** (See Figure 13) is of a triangular form. It arises from the convexity of the hook of the unciform bone and contiguous portion of the annular ligament; its fibers pass downward and inward, to be inserted into the whole length of the metacarpal bone of the little finger along its ulnar margin.

Action: The opponens minimi digiti draws forward the fifth metacarpal bone, so as to deepen the hollow of the palm.

The **opponens pollicis** (See Figure 13), is a small triangular muscle. It arises from the palmar surface of the ridge on the trapezium and from the annular ligament, passes downward and outward, and is inserted into the whole length of the metacarpal bone of the thumb on its radial side.

Action: It flexes the metacarpal bone, that is, draws it inward and over the palm - and at the same time, rotates the bone, so as to turn the thumb toward the finger, thus producing the movement of opposition.

The **flexor minimi digiti brevis** (See Figure 13), arises from the transverse carpal ligament and the hamulus of the hamate bone. It inserts at the ulnar side and base of the proximal phalanx of the little finger.

Action: It assists in flexing the proximal phalanx of the little finger.

The **flexor pollicis brevis** (See Figure 13), originates at the transverse carpal ligament and the trapezium bone. It terminates at the base of the proximal phalanx of the thumb.

Action: The flexor pollicis brevis flexes and adducts the proximal phalanx of the thumb.

The **palmar interossei** (See Figure 13), are three small muscles found on the palmar surface of the metacarpal bones. They arise from the entire length of the metacarpal bone of one finger, and are inserted into the base of the first phalanx. The *first* arises from the ulnar side of the second metacarpal bone, and is inserted into the same side of the first phalanx of the index finger. The *second* arises from the radial side of the fourth metacarpal bone and is inserted into the same side of the ring finger. The *third* arises from the radial side of the fifth metacarpal bone, and is inserted into the same side of the little finger.

Action: The palmar interossei muscles adduct the fingers to an imaginary line drawn longitudinally through the center of the middle finger.

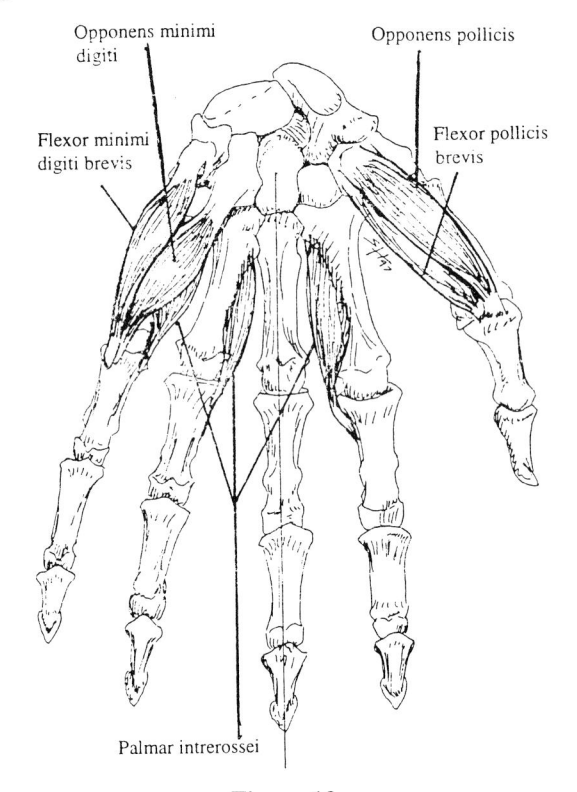

Figure 13

The **adductor pollicis** (See Figure 14), arises by two heads. The oblique head from the bases of the second and third metacarpal bones. From this origin the greater number of fibers pass obliquely downward and converge into a tendon. It is inserted into the inner side of the base of the first phalanx of the thumb. The transverse head is of triangular form and arises from the lower two-third of the metacarpal bone of the middle finger on its palmar surface. The fibers proceed outward, converge, and are inserted into the ulnar side of the base of the first phalanx of the thumb.

The **first dorsal interosseous** (See Figure 14), muscle is larger than the others. It is flat, triangular in form, and arises by two heads, separated by a fiberous arch. The outer head arises from the upper half of the ulnar border of the first metacarpal bone; the inner head, from almost the entire length of the radial border of the second metacarpal bone. The tendon is inserted into the radial side of the index finger.

Action of the adductor pollicis and the interosseous:

The adductor pollicis adducts the thumb and works in concert with the first dorsal interosseous muscle in grasping an object between the thumb and index finger.

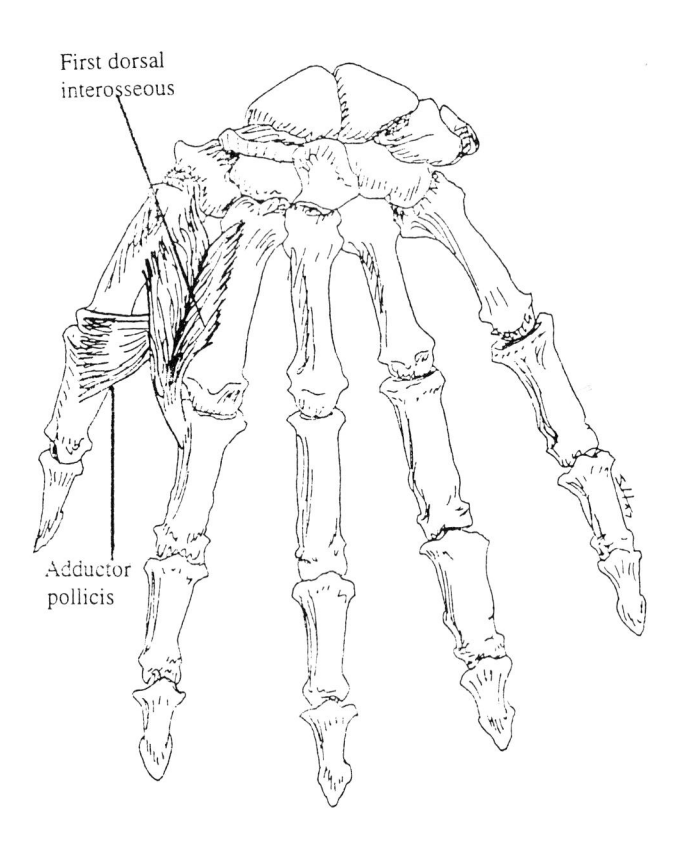

Figure 14

Exercise No. 6

1) In each hand grip a golf ball with your thumb, index finger and middle finger as if to throw it. With arms hanging naturally at your side observe the back of your left hand and the palm of your right hand. **Photo 13**

2) Bring your thumbs and little fingers together in front of you and move the hands up and down like hammering. **Photos 14 & 15**

3) Now place the ulnar edge of your right hand on the radial edge of the first bone of the left thumb. Repeat the up and down movements. **Photo 16**

4) Observe very carefully the position of your right middle finger.

Exercise No. 6   Step 1   Photo 13

Exercise No. 6   Step 2   Photo 14

Exercise No. 6   Step 2   Photo 15

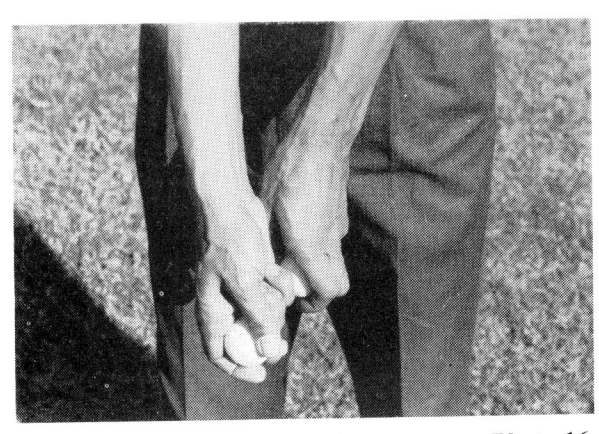

Exercise No. 6   Step 3   Photo 16

How to achieve the **Seven Digit Grip**

Exercise No 7.

The Correct Left Hand Grip:

1) Repeat Steps 1 thru 3 of Exercise No. 1. with your arms hanging naturally at your sides.

2) Hold the grip of the club in your left hand similar to the way you held the golf ball in Step 1 of Exercise No. 6. **Photo 17**

3) The sole of the club is flat on the ground, not on the toe or heel. The club is held so that the shaft runs across the base of your last three fingers and is encircled by the thumb. When you look down, at least three knuckles on the back of your left hand will be seen. **Photo 17**

Exercise No. 7   Steps 2 & 3   Photo 17

The Correct Right Hand Grip:

1) Bend your right knee slightly, as you did in Step 6 of Exercise No. 1. **Photo 18**

2) Naturally swing your right hand across your thighs until it reaches the club. **DO NOT MOVE YOUR LEFT HAND AT ALL. Photo 18**

3) When your right hand reaches the club, the ulnar edge of your right palm is rested against the first bone of your encircling left thumb. Similar to Step 3 of Exercise No. 6. **Photos 19 & 20**

4) Hold the grip of the club with the thumb, index finger and middle finger of your right hand. Similar to the way you held the golf ball in Step 1 of Exercise No. 6. **Photos 19 & 20**

5) The little finger on your right hand may overlap, interlock or rest against the index finger on your left hand.

6) Apply a firm and even amount of pressure with the last three fingers and thumb of your left hand and an adequate but lighter pressure with the index finger, middle finger and thumb of the right hand. One knuckle on the back of your right hand is visible.

ANATOMY OF THE PERFECT GOLF SWING   GLENNON E. BAZZLE

Exercise No. 7   Step 4   Photo 18

Exercise No. 7   Steps 3 & 4 Photo 20

Exercise No. 7   Steps 3 & 4 Photo 19

Exercise No. 8

1) Assume the correct left hand and right hand grip.

2) Stand erect. Bend your right elbow so it rests on the iliac crest of the pelvic bone, or into your right side. **Photo 21**

3) With your left arm still straight, pronate or turn the left arm to the right, making an arc with the club head down towards your right knee. This exercise strengthens your pronators and the prime movers of your wrist in the up-back swing. Add this action to the end of Step 2 of Exercise No. 5 **Photos 22 & 23**

Exercise No. 8   Step 2   Photo 21

ANATOMY OF THE PERFECT GOLF SWING   GLENNON E. BAZZLE

Exercise No. 8   Step 3   Photo 22

Exercise No. 8   Step 3   Photo 23

We can now return to the other prime movers in the forearm.

The prime movers of the forearm articulation between the radius and the ulna bones in the golf swing are the Pronator Radii Teres and the Pronator Quadratus. (See Figure 15).

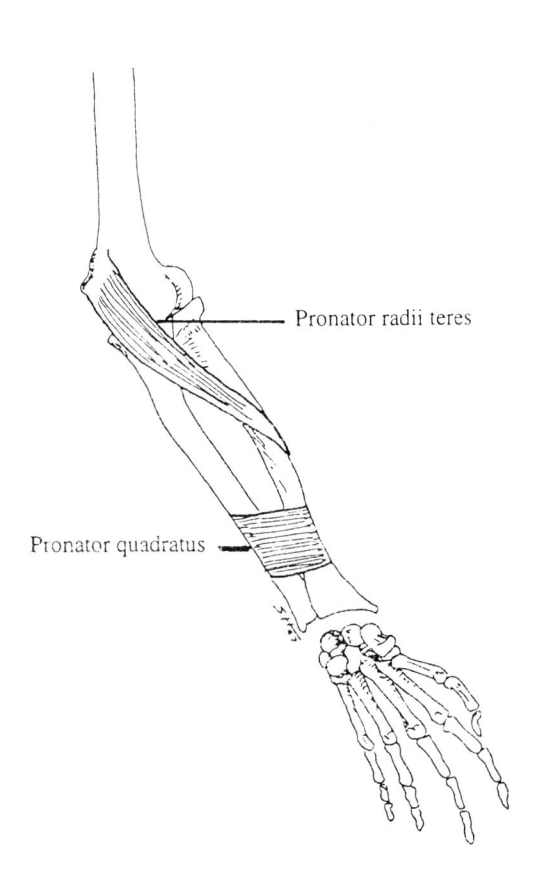

Figure 15

The **pronator radii teres** arises by two heads. One, the larger and more superficial, arises from the humerus, immediately above the external condyle, and the other head is a thin fasciculus which arises from the inner side of the coronoid process of the ulna joining the preceding at an acute angle. The muscle passes obliquely across the forearm from the inner to the outer side, and terminates in a flat tendon, which turns over the outer margin of the radius, and is inserted into a rough impression at the middle of the outer surface of the shaft of that bone.

Action: The Pronator Radii-Teres helps to rotate the radius upon the ulna, rendering the hand prone.

The **pronator quadratus** is a small, flat, quadrilateral muscle, extending transversely across the front of the radius and ulna, above their carpal extremities. It arises from the oblique or pronator ridge on the lower part of the anterior surface of the shaft of the ulna. The fiber passes outward and slightly downward to be inserted into the lower fourth of the anterior surface and anterior border of the shaft of the radius.

Action: The Pronator Quadratus helps rotate the radius upon the ulna, rendering the hand prone.

The Inferior Radio-Ulnar Articulation

This is also a pivot joint, formed by the head of the ulna received into the sigmoid cavity of the inner side of the lower end of the radius. The articular surface is covered by a thin layer of cartilage, and connected together by two ligaments, the anterior radio-ulnar and the posterior radio-ulnar. The anterior radio-ulnar ligament is a narrow band of fibers extending from the anterior margin of the sigmoid cavity of the radius to the anterior surface of the head of the ulna. The posterior radio-ulnar ligament extends between similar points on the posterior surface of the articulation.

Joint Action

The movement of the inferior radio-ulnar articulation is just the reverse of that in the superior radio-ulnar joint. It consists of a movement of rotation of the lower end of the radius around an axis which corresponds to the center of the head of the ulna. When the radius rotates forward, pronation of the forearm and hand is the result, and when backward, supination. It will thus be seen that in pronation and supination of the forearm and hand, the radius describes a segment of a cone, the axis of which extends from the center of the head of the radius to the middle of the head of the ulna.

The Prime Movers Of The Wrist In The Back-Upward Swing

The prime movers for us are the Flexor Carpi Radialis and the Extensor Carpi Radialis Longus and Brevis.

The **flexor carpi radialis** (See Figure 16-a), arises from the internal condyle of the humerus by a common tendon and from the fascia of the forearm. It is slender and aponeurotic in structure at its beginning, it increases in size, and terminates in a tendon which forms rather more than half of its lower length. This tendon is inserted into the base of the metacarpal bone of the index finger, and by a slip into the base of the metacarpal bone of the middle finger.

Action: The flexor carpi radialis is one of the flexors of the wrist; when acting alone, it flexes the wrist, inclining it to the radial side, abduction.

The **extensor carpi radialis longus** (See Figure 16-b), originates on the lower third of the lateral supracondylar ridge of the humerus and the lateral intermuscular septum. The fibers terminate at the upper third of the forearm in a flat tendon, which runs along the outer border of the radius. It is inserted into the base of the metacarpal bone of the index finger, on its radial side.

Action: The extensor carpi radialis longus extends the wrist and abducts the hand.

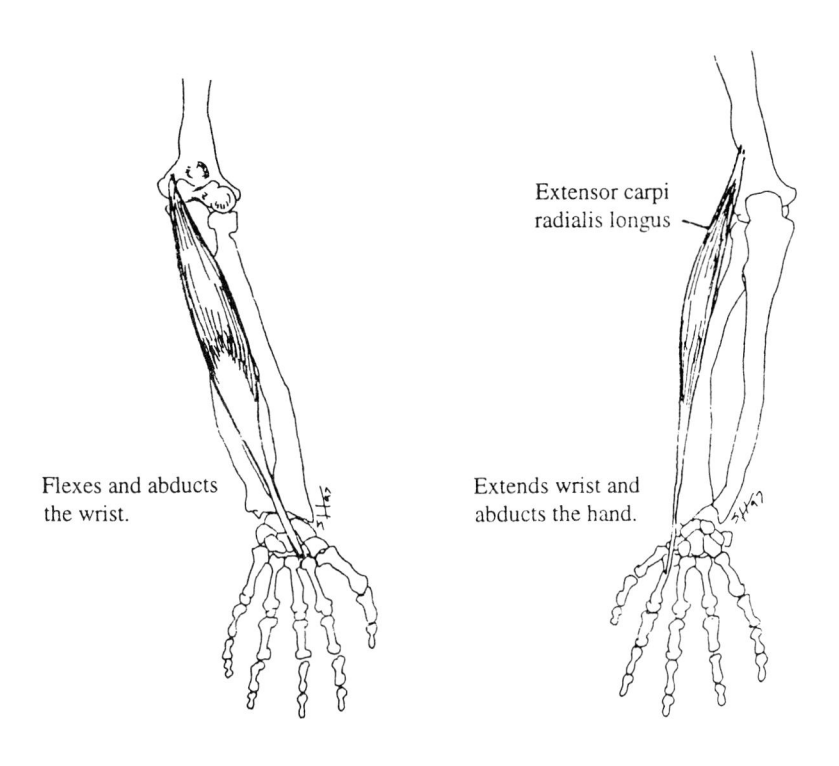

Flexes and abducts the wrist.

Extensor carpi radialis longus

Extends wrist and abducts the hand.

Figure 16a   **Figure 16b**

The **extensor carpi radialis brevis** (See Figure 16-c), is shorter, as the name implies, and thicker than the preceding muscle, beneath which it is placed. It arises from a common extensor tendon from the lateral epicondyle of the humerus. The fibers terminate about the middle of the forearm in a flat tendon which is closely connected with that of the preceding muscle, and accompanies it to the wrist. It diverges somewhat from it's fellow, and is inserted into the base of the metacarpal bone of the middle finger, on its radial side.

Action: The extensor carpi radialis brevis assists the extensor carpi radialis longus in extending the wrist, and may also act slightly as an abductor of the hand.

Extends wrist and abducts the hand

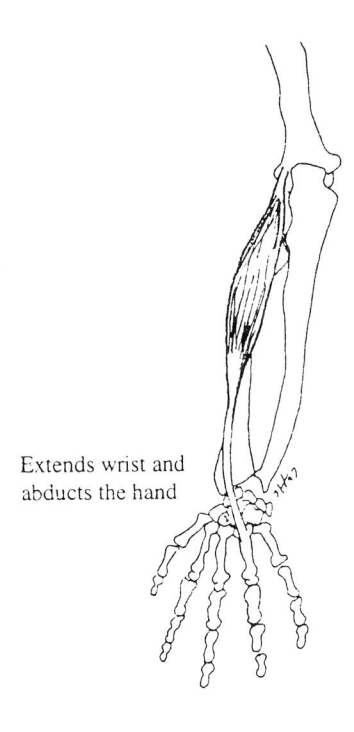

Figure 16c

You now know all of the bones, the joints they form, the muscles, tendons, and ligaments that move them, completing the back-upward swing. When you master these few simple movements, in the proper sequence, you will have successfully completed the winding up motion needed to release centrifugal force in the golf swing. My friend, that is the **BACK-UPWARD SWING.**

CONGRATULATIONS!!!!!!!!

TAKE A BREAK. YOU DESERVE IT.

HOW TO RELEASE CENTRIFUGAL FORCE ON YOUR CENTER OF GRAVITY

THE DOWN-FORWARD SWING

The proper back-upward portion of the swing has been successfully executed. It has maintained our fulcrum or central theme, which is to satisfy the definition of centrifugal force, by always moving away from the center of rotation, hip, back, chest, shoulder, arm, wrists and fingers. We must now move our attention away from the little prime movers that wound up the body to the larger muscles that were antagonists and being stretched in the winding up motion. They are now the prime movers of the down-forward swing. **Note: The sequence of the unwinding process is the hip, back, chest, shoulder, arm, and wrists.**

The large muscles that have been *"stretched"* in the windup are the Trapezius, Latissimus Dorsi, the Teres Major, and the Posterior Fibers of the Deltoid. The Triceps, the Anconeus, the Extensor Carpi Ulnaris and the Flexor Carpi. These muscles have been systematically stretched in the wind up and are now ready to be released. Remember when we reviewed the characteristics of muscles we noticed that muscles that have been stretched or contracted reacted in the same manner. Because of elasticity, they have the ability to **"bounce back"**. And so what is commonly referred to as the "point of impact" in the golf swing is really **"the point of maximum contraction of the extensor muscles"**.

The Trapezius

The **trapezius** (See Figure 17) is broad, flat, triangular, placed immediately beneath the skin and fascia, and covering the upper and back part of the neck and shoulders. It arises from the inner third of the superior curved line of the occipital bone; the spinous process of the seventh cervical, and those of all the dorsal vertebrae. From this origin the superior fibers proceed downward and outward, the inferior ones upward and outward, and the middle fibers horizontally. The superior ones are inserted into the outer third of the posterior border of the clavicle. The middle fibers insert into the inner margin of the acromion process. The inner fibers converge near the scapula, and terminate in a triangular aponeurosis, which glides over a smooth surface at the inner extremity of the spine, to be inserted into a tubercle at the outer part of this smooth surface.

Action: The whole of the trapezius when in action retracts the scapula and braces back the shoulder. If the head is fixed, the upper part of the trapezius will elevate the point of the shoulder, as in supporting weights. The middle and lower fibers of the muscle rotate the scapula, causing elevation of the acromion process.

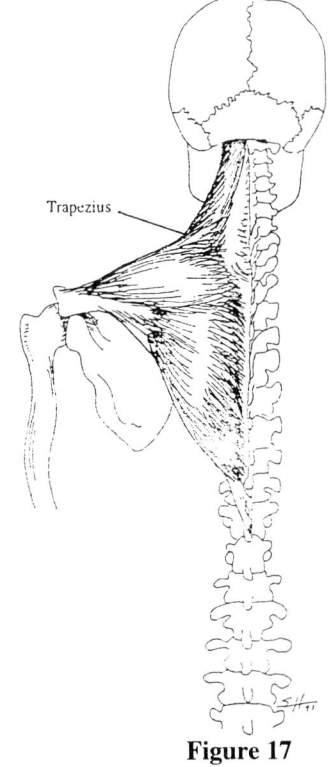

Figure 17

The Latissimus Dorsi

The **latissimus dorsi** (See Figure 18), is a broad flat superficial muscle which covers the lower half of the back. Its origin spans from about the seventh thoracic vertebra to the ilium. From this extensive origin the fibers pass in different directions, the upper ones horizontally, the middle obliquely upward, and the lower vertically upward so as to converge and form a thick fasciculus. The muscle is twisted upon itself so that the superior fibers become at first posterior and then inferior, and the vertical fibers at first anterior and then superior. It then terminates into a short quadrilateral tendon, about three inches long, and is inserted into the bottom of the bicipital groove of the humerus.

Action: This muscle is a powerful extensor of the arm. One of its actions upon the arm is to draw it backward. It is also the muscle which is principally used in giving a downward blow, as in chopping a tree or swinging a golf club.

The Teres Major

The **teres major** (See Figure 18), is a superficial muscle that originates on the dorsal surface of the inferior angle of the scapula. Its insertion is on the medial lip of the bicipital groove of the humerus. It lies near its companion, the latissimus dorsi, at the inferior angle of the scapula. Rounded mass of the teres major can be readily palpated near the upper border of the latissimus dorsi. The teres major courses upward paralleling the latissimus dorsi until the latter spirals around it. The muscle inserts by a broad tendon in close juxtaposition to its partner on the medial aspect of the humerus.

Action: It assists the latissimus dorsi in extending the arm.

The Posterior Fibers Of The Deltoid

The description of the deltoid has already been given. (See Figure 18).

Action: The posterior fibers aid the latissimus dorsi and the teres major in drawing the arm back.

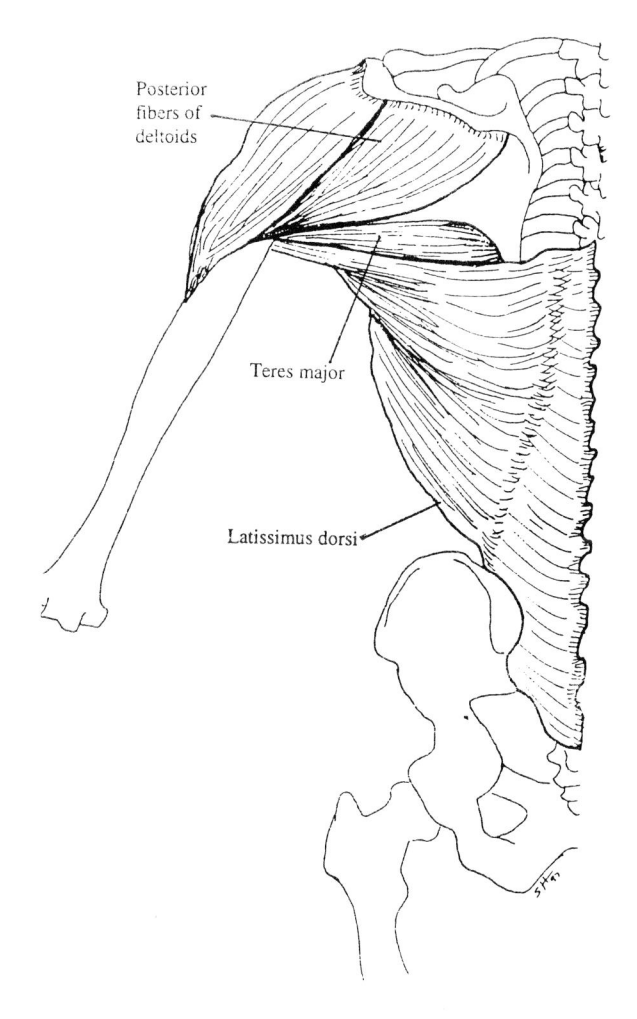

Figure 18

The Triceps Brachii

The **triceps brachii** (See Figure 19), is a three headed muscle that makes up the posterior aspect of the humerus. The long head originates from the infra glenoid tuberosity of the scapula. The lateral head's origin is at the posterior and the lateral surface of the humerus, and the medial head which origin is on the lower posterior surface of the humerus. They insert at the upper posterior surface of the olecranon and deep fascia of the forearm. The long and lateral heads of the triceps brachii may be observed and palpated on the posterior aspect of the arm, when performing elbow extension. The long head is observed emerging from beneath the posterior fibers of the deltoid, with the tendons of the latissimus dorsi and the teres major below. The lateral head of the muscle is clearly delineated from the deltoid, superiorly. The medial head may be felt distally on the arm near the medial epicondyle. Insignificant muscle, anconeus, appears as a continuation of the medial head of the triceps near the lateral epicondyle continuing on to the ulna. The anconeus may be considered a functional part of the triceps brachii.

Action: The triceps brachii is a great extensor of the forearm, extending the elbow-joint. When the arm is extended the long head of the muscle may assist the teres major and latissimus dorsi in drawing the humerus backward.

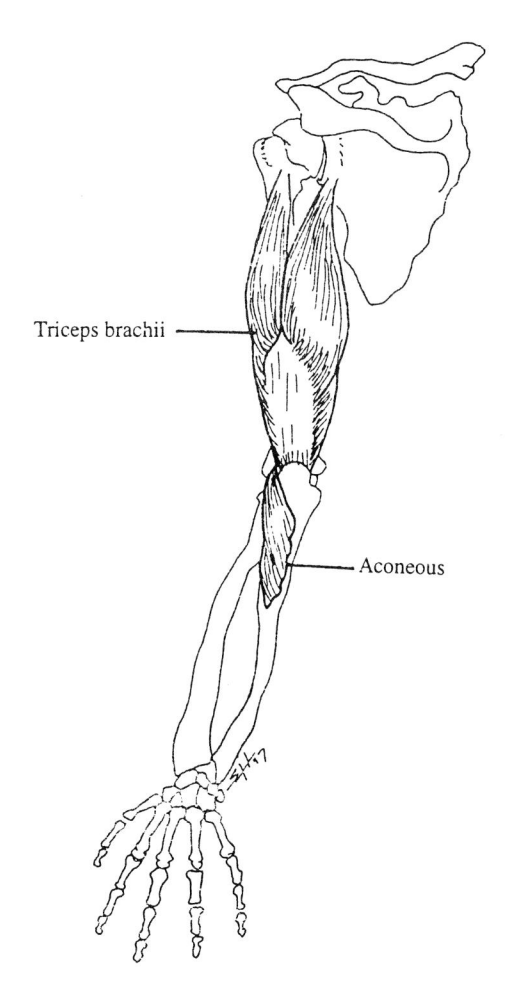

Figure 19

The Extensor Carpi Ulnaris

The **extensor carpi ulnaris** (See Figure 20-a), is the most superficial muscle on the ulnar side of the forearm. It arises from the external condyle of the humerus by a common tendon, and from the posterior border of the ulna. This muscle terminates in a tendon which is inserted into the prominent tubercle on the ulnar side of the base of the metacarpal bone of the little finger.

Action: It extends the hand; acting alone it inclines it toward the ulnar side; it also extends the elbow-joint.

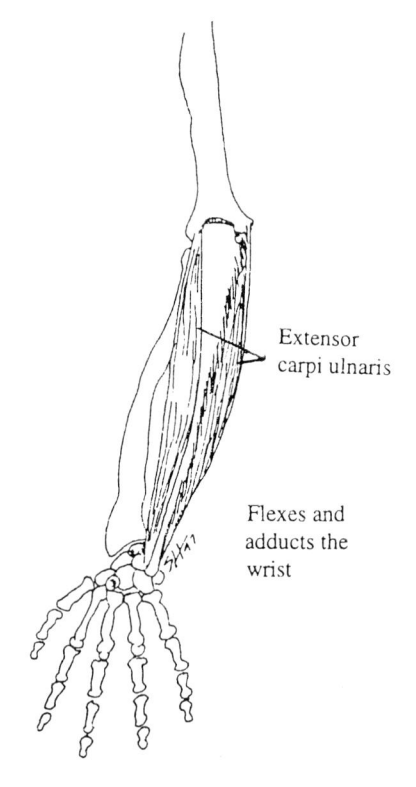

Figure 20-a

The Flexor Carpi Ulnaris

The **flexor carpi ulnaris** (See Figure 20-b), lies along the ulnar side of the forearm. It arises by two heads, connected by a tendinous arch. One head arises from the inner condyle of the humerus by the common tendon; the other from the inner margin of the olecranon and from the upper two-thirds of the posterior border of the ulna by an aponeurosis. The fibers terminate in a tendon which occupies the anterior part of the lower half of the muscle, and is inserted into the pisiform bone, and is prolonged from this to the fifth metacarpal and unciform bones.

Action: The flexor carpi ulnaris is a flexor of the wrist, inclining it to the ulnar side.

Flexor carpi ulnaris

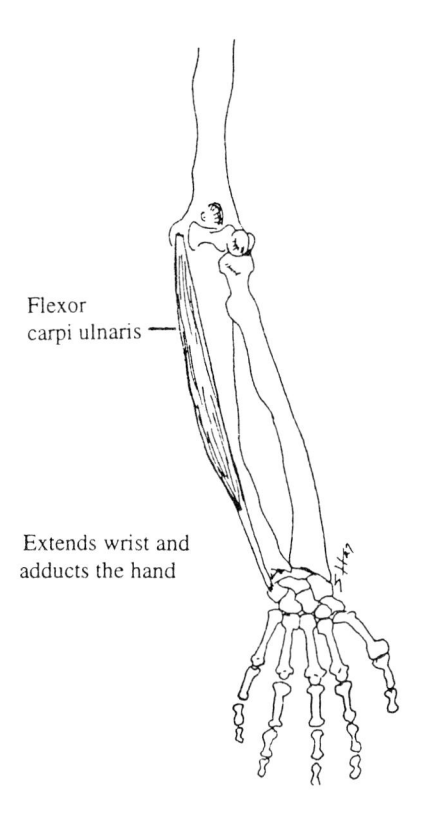

Extends wrist and adducts the hand

Figure 20-b

Now you know all the large muscles that were stretched during the back-upward swing. They should reach maximum contraction at the point of impact during the down-forward swing.

CONGRATULATIONS AGAIN!!!!!!!

THE MENTAL ASPECT OF THE GOLF SWING

Here is another definition. **Consciousness--the quality or state of being aware, especially of something within oneself.** That being the case, you must be very deliberate, but not slow, and totally aware of making the back-upward movements in the correct sequential order. **Hip, back, chest, shoulder, arm, and wrist.** However, once the left hip initiates the down-forward swing the rest of the unwinding process happens too quickly to try to control it consciously. And speaking of consciousness, let us now turn our attention to the **Mental Aspect** of the swing.

In keeping with our central theme of working from the center of rotation outwardly on the physical aspects of the swing we must do the same with the mental aspect. And to do so properly we must do as we did with the physical aspect. By examining the bones, joints and muscles we got a better and clearer understanding of how they function. Now we have to examine the organ from which that better and clearer understanding comes. It is at the center of all golfers. That organ is the **brain**.

The brain is that portion of the cerebro-spinal axis which is contained in the cavity of the cranium. For the persons who are interested in pursuing deeper into the structure and function of the brain, I encourage you to do so. But, for our purpose I will be brief in my explanation of the mental aspect of the golf swing.

The brain has two hemispheres or sides. A left side, whose functions includes reading, writing, speaking, problem solving, analyzing, rational thinking, and concentration. And, a right side whose functions include dreaming, fantasizing, imagination, and visualization. As you can see each side has its own functions, which allows them to work independently of each other at the same time; one side only, or both sides working together on the same idea at the same time, and unfortunately, to often, in conflict with each other. In our left brain dominated society it's difficult to shut down the left brain long enough to really appreciate and understand what the right brain has to offer. In golf, as in most successful endeavors, both left brain and right brain are working together on the same swing image at the same time.

There is certainly a mental activity in the golf swing. Many think that it is concentration. They are partially correct. Concentration is a left brain function. Imagination, on the other hand is a right brain function. Before executing the actual physical swing, you must see clearly in your mind (**image-in,** using right brain) the shape of the swing you wish to make, where to stand to align yourself properly so the club can draw the imaginary line the ball will fly on to the landing area. After you have visualized what to do, the left side can now make its contribution by making a logical, rational, and tactical decision as to which club to use to execute the swing.

THE BIG TRICK

The big trick is in keeping the shape of the swing in mind, a right brain function, and convincing the left brain that it will not lose its dominance, but that you need its cooperation to be still just long enough to allow you to make the swing. Sounds easy enough? Sure. Truly it is easy. At first it may seem strange telling the left brain not to get involved. You'll probably find yourself, left brain that is, thinking of something other than the image when and while you are swinging the club. But after a while, with practice, when it, left brain, becomes convinced that it has not been left out all together, and it begins to see the positive results, left brain will not only become more comfortable and cooperative with its subordinate role, for a milli-second or so, it will start to take credit for the success of the swing based on its ability to be still.

I now offer three variations of a similar idea hoping that you will remember one.

1) If you think of an action without a conflicting thought, your body will perform it. Psychologists describe this as ideo-motor action. First there is an idea- and then the motor mechanism of your body, guided by your subconscious mind, carries it out in intricate detail without any further thought on your part.

2) I quote from the late, great, Harvey Penick, in his book with Bud Shrake, 1995, For All Who Love the Game, Lessons and Teachings for Women. "If you see the shot in your mind, your muscles will do their best to make it happen. One of the biggest differences between high-handicap players and good players is the picture show of the mind. The good player visualizes the shot. Each and every shot. The good player sees in the mind where the ball will fly and how it will land, and thus subconsciously instruct

the muscles what is wanted. The high handicapper doesn't. Your imagination is an important aspect of the game. USE IT".

3) And this one I call "THE OTHER SIDE OF THE WALL". You must imagine the swing in your head. Imagine it shaped and balanced the way you want it. Get it in your head and then believe in it. Visualize it, believe it, and your body will do it. Any swing you can imagine clearly, your body can make. THAT IS THE GREAT SECRET. IT GOES BEYOND THE BODY.

HOW TO SYNTHESIZE THE BACK-UPWARD SWING AND THE DOWN-FORWARD SWING

Now that we have analyzed the bones, joints, muscles, tendons, and ligaments involved in both the back-upward swing and the down-forward swing; learned exercises to develop those muscles; learned the proper sequence to move these muscles; plus looked at the brain to see how it works in regards to the golf swing, we are now ready to put all of this information together and synthesize the swing.

To synthesize the golf swing we must blend all of the parts together in a certain sequence.

THE BACK-UPWARD SWING

1) Assume the proper left hand grip and the proper right hand grip exactly how they were described and the way you have practiced gripping the club. Do not move your left hand, or pick up the club to meet the right hand. This method of gripping the club automatically squares the back of your left hand and the palm of your right hand with the club face. Emphasis should be placed on the proper amount of pressure on the **"Seven Digits"**. **Firm and even pressure with the little, ring, and middle fingers and thumb of your left hand; and adequate and lighter pressure with the index finger, middle finger and thumb of your right hand. Remember the left thumb encircles the club.**

By gripping the club in this manner the ankle, knee, hip, shoulder, elbow and wrist on the right side of your body are flexed, while their counterparts on the left side are extended. You are in a similar position at address and at impact.

2) Stand erect, aim your chin at a point directly opposite the center of your body, heels about shoulder width apart and toes pointed outwardly about 30 degrees. **Photo 24**

3) Find your center of gravity, distribute weight evenly. About 50% on each side of your midline. Shift 25% of your weight to the left side of your body. This is easily done by slightly bending the right knee. Now you have 75% of your weight on the left side and must feel the weight between the ball and heel (a bit more toward the heel) of your left foot. **Photo 24**

4) Extend the arms placing the sole of the club on the ground with its face squared to the intended line of flight. **Photo 24**

5) Simply shift your weight back to the right side of the body. The left knee will bend slightly inward, and then 75% of your weight should be felt between the ball and heel (a bit more toward the heel) of your right foot. This action automatically moves the club about six inches to the right and inside the point where your chin is aimed. The right **gluteus maximus** and **medius** stabilize and support the trunk and the entire lower right limb is now properly grounded and you will have perfect balance and leverage throughout the swing. Now you can turn on your right hip joint. (**The lateral rotators**). **Photos 25 and 26**

6) Turn the upper left side of the shoulder girdle towards the midline. **The Key.** I wonder if you were paying attention when I told you that the word (clavicle) comes from the word clavis which means **KEY**. **When the left multifidus spinae, the rotators of the dorsal region of the spine, the left pectoralis minor and the left serratus anterior contract, they cause this turn.** *Note: (The upper fibers of the left trapezius which are inserted into the clavicle assist in turning the shoulder toward the midline).* **The clavicle turns on the sternum until the outer end of the shoulder comes under the chin**. This movement positions the body so the arms are allowed to swing unimpeded. In this position you will have achieved both, the proper or full hip turn and the proper shoulder turn. **Photo 27**

7) Raise the left arm. Up to this point the proper hip and shoulder turns have been responsible for moving the club back and upward without any deliberate effort on your part. When the proper shoulder turn nears its completion, **the coracoid brachialis and the anterior fibers of the deltoid raise the left humerus, which articulates within the glenoid fossa of the scapula.** **Photo 28**

8) That is followed by the **radio-ulnar articulation.** The proper left hand grip causes your left **pronator radii teres and the left pronator quadratus** to be in a semi-pronated position. As you continue raising your left arm the rest of pronation is completed, and the right elbow is kept comfortably near your right side. At this point the **flexor carpi radialis and extensor carpi radialis** of both arms contract, causing your wrists to cock over and behind your right shoulder. This causes the face of the club to open and the nose to point toward the ground. **Photo 28**

That concludes the back-upward swing or the winding up process. Each component must be allowed to perform its skill in the proper sequence without any omissions, incompletions, or interruptions if you expect to effectively achieve accuracy and consistency efficiently.

THE DOWN-FORWARD SWING

9) The down-forward swing is started by shifting your weight back to the left side. The **left gluteus maximus** and **medius** stabilize the limb and support the trunk. The **left lateral rotators** turn your left hip back to the left. **Photo 30**

10) The **left lateral** and **inferior fibers** of the **trapezius** contract, retracting and stabilizing the left shoulder blade so the glenoid fossa is still facing forward and left arm can properly perform circumduction. **Photo 31**

11) When your **latissimus dorsi, teres major** and **posterior fibers of the deltoid** on the left side of your body contract, these powerful extensors extend the humerus down and forward. **Photo 32**

12) Your left **triceps brachii** extends the forearm. Later, together with the **lateral fibers of the deltoid** they assist in the lateral extension of your left humerus. **Photo 33**

13) Finally, the **extensor carpi ulnaris** and the **flexor carpi ulnaris** of both arms contract at the same time, causing the wrists to **"uncock"** and extend your (**one new hand**) on both extended forearms, thus "locking the elbows" at impact. This is called **"perfect timing"**. **Photo 34**

14) The follow through and the finish are accomplished basically by the continuous stretching of the left **latissimus dorsi** and the **lower fiber of the trapezius** as they try to raise the left arm to a vertical position. The right side of the shoulder girdle follows the lead of the left extensors and is pulled under the chin. **REMEMBER: THE POINT OF IMPACT IS WHERE THE EXTENSOR MUSCLES THAT HAVE BEEN "STRETCHED" ARE "CONTRACTED", AND THE SWING MUST CONTINUE UNTIL THE HANDS REACH A POINT NEAR OR OVER THE LEFT SHOULDER).** That is it. You have successfully **created and released centrifugal force on your center of gravity**. Wind up properly, and don't interfere with the unwinding. **Photos 35.**

"THE GOLF SWING IS A MATTER OF TRUSTING YOUR IMAGINATION"

CONGRATULATIONS AND GOOD PLAYING!!!!

Prime Movers: Muscles of grip in hands and arms
Photo 24   **Steps 2, 3, & 4**

Prime Mover: Right lateral rotators
Photo 26   **Step 5**

Prime Mover: Right gluteus maximus and medius
Photo 25   **Step 5**

Prime Movers: Left multifidus spinae, rotators, spinae, pectoralis minor, serratus anterior, upper left fibers of trapezius
Photo 27   **Step 6**

ANATOMY OF THE PERFECT GOLF SWING GLENNON E. BAZZLE

Prime Movers: Left coracoid brachialis and anterior fibers of the deltoid.
Prime Movers: Left Pronator radii teres, pronator quadratus. flexor carpi radialis and extensor carpi radialis longus and brevis
Photo 28 **Steps 7 & 8**

Prime Movers: Lattissimus dorsi, teres major and posterior fibers of the deltoid
Photo 30 **Step 11**

Prime Movers: Left gluteus maximus and medius and lateral rotators.
Prime Movers: Left lateral and inferior fibers of trapezius.
Photo 29 **Steps 9 & 10**

Prime Removers: Triceps, brachii and aconeous.
Photo 31 **Step 12**

74

ANATOMY OF THE PERFECT GOLF SWING　　　　GLENNON E. BAZZLE

Prime Movers: Extensor carpi ulnaris, flexor carpi ulnaris
Photo 32　　　　　　　　　Step 13

Photo 34　　　　　　　　　Step 14

Prime Movers: Latissimus dorsi and lower fibers of trapezius
Photo 33　　　　　　　　　Step 14

Photo 35　　　　　　　　　Step 14

NOTES

GLOSSARY OF KEY TERMS

(Note: Terms listed in the order of appearance in text).

PERFECT GOLF SWING- The **perfect golf swing** is one complete, smooth, flowing motion without any emotional, mental or physical interruptions.   (Page 2)

LEVER- a rigid bar that moves about a fixed point.   (Page 6)

CENTRIFUGAL FORCE- is the force that an object moving along a circular path exerts on the body constraining the object and that acts outwardly away from the center of rotation.   (Page 7)

CENTER OF GRAVITY- is the point in your body around which your weight is evenly distributed or balanced and may be assumed to act.   (Page 8)

ROTATION- to spin or turn.   (Page 35)

FLEXION- to decrease the angle of a joint.   (Page 35)

EXTENSION- to increase the angle of a joint.   (Page 35)

ADDUCTION- to bring toward the body.   (Page 35)

ABDUCTION- to move away from the body.   (Page 35)

CIRCUMDUCTION- is a combination of rotation, flexion, extension, adduction and abduction; and while it is being performed the distal end moves along a circular path.   (Page 35)

GRIP- the act of taking firmly and holding fast with the hands.   (Page 36)

CONSCIOUSNESS- the quality or state of being aware, especially of something within oneself.   (Page 65)

Reference

Gray's Anatomy. Dr. Henry Gray. Bounty Books 1927

---———— **NOTES** ————---

Mr. Bazzle is available to share his knowledge, expertise and experience in enhancing your application of the Perfect Golf Swing through seminars, workshops, individual or group lessons and private consultations.

Order extra copies of

Anatomy of the Perfect Golf Swing from:

Lobdell and Potter Publishers
6900 Curran Road
New Orleans, Louisiana 70126
Phone: (504) 243-0322   Fax: (504) 243-0322
e-mail BAZZLINE@aol.com

NOTES

NOTES

NOTES